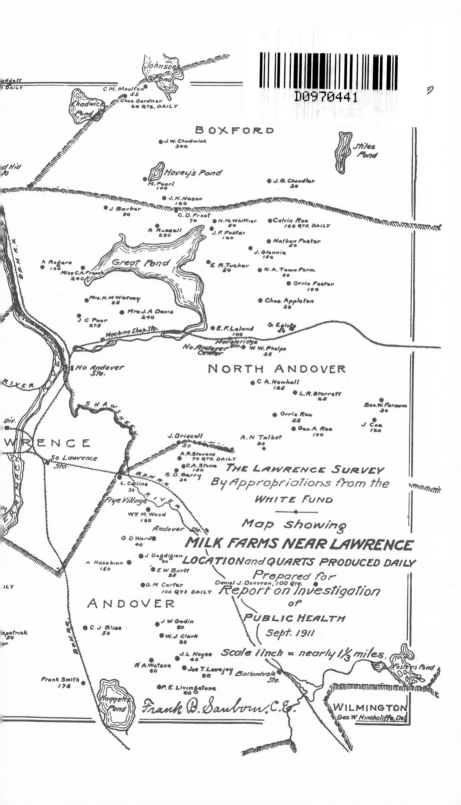

THE LAWRENCE SURVEY
By Appropriations from the
WHITE FUND

Map showing
MILK FARMS NEAR LAWRENCE
LOCATION and QUARTS PRODUCED DAILY
Prepared for
Report on Investigation
of
PUBLIC HEALTH
Sept. 1911

Scale 1 inch = nearly 1½ miles.

Frank B. Sanborn, C.E.

FIVE THOUSAND DAYS
LIKE THIS ONE

A CONCORD LIBRARY BOOK

John Elder, series editor

ALSO BY JANE BROX

Here and Nowhere Else:
Late Seasons of a Farm and Its Family

Five Thousand Days
Like This One

AN AMERICAN FAMILY HISTORY

Jane Brox

BEACON PRESS · BOSTON

Beacon Press
25 Beacon Street
Boston, Massachusetts 02108-2892
www.beacon.org

Beacon Press books
are published under the auspices of
the Unitarian Universalist Association of Congregations.

Text design by Charles Nix
Set in Nix Rift
Composition by Wilsted & Taylor Publishing Services

Excerpts from *The Last Generation: Work and Life in the Textile Mills of
Lowell, Massachusetts, 1910–1960*, by Mary H. Blewett (Amherst: University of
Massachusetts Press, 1990), are reprinted by permission of University of Massachu-
setts Press. Copyright © 1990 by the University of Massachusetts Press.

Excerpts from *Amoskeag* by Tamara K. Hareven and Randoph Langenbach.
Copyright © 1978 by Tamara Hareven. Reprinted by permission of Pantheon
Books, a division of Random House, Inc.

Excerpt from the taped interview of Ernie Russell from the collection of the Immigrant City Archives, Lawrence, Massachusetts, is reprinted by permission of the
Immigrant City Archives.

Excerpt from "At the Fishhouses" from *The Complete Poems 1927–1979* by
Elizabeth Bishop. Copyright © 1979, 1983 by Alice Helen Methfessel. Reprinted
by permission of Farrar, Straus, and Giroux, Inc.

Library of Congress Cataloging-in-Publication Data can be found on p. 184.

IN MEMORIAM:
John Brox
1910–1995

CONTENTS

I

I I

I I I

I

. . . whether the hills will look as blue as the sailors say.

—Emily Dickinson

1

Afterwards

IT HAD BEEN A DROUGHTY SUMMER. THE OR-
chard grasses turned sere by late June, the brook beds shrunk
to dried mud, and the apples reached no more than half their
best size. The worst of them—ones marked up with codling
moth scars or scab—weren't even worth hauling to the apple
cellar. Strange to see bushel after bushel of Cortland, Mc-
Intosh, and Northern Spies in heaps under the trees. Even
stranger was the way the sweet smell of those fermenting
apples drew the deer out of the woods—more deer than anyone in living memory had ever seen here. They'd forage
through the fallen leaves under the bare crowns of the trees,
coming more and more frequently as the apples frosted and
thawed by turns down the shortening autumn days until they
froze through at last and were covered with an early December snow.

Through the first quiet winter storms, the deer stayed in
the part of the orchard that bordered the woods, nosing the
snow near the apple bark, raising their heads every now and
again, wary, listening. But as the snow deepened they came
further into the orchard, and I could trace their tracks from
tree to tree. They came at all hours—nine of them once—fil-

ing along the edge of the pines at eleven in the morning on a cloudless day. Even my father, who'd seen them all his life, remarked: "Look at that. In broad daylight."

We talked about them every day as I stopped by my parents' house in the late afternoon, my mother in the kitchen, my father at his desk going over the farm year on paper:

"I saw three under the Cortland trees, one couldn't have been more than a yearling."

"Is that so? They must be finding apples still. I hope they don't start grazing on the branches."

"Oh, you think?"

As long as the deer kept to the fallen apples, they stood clear of any concern of ours. Just beautiful things even for the hunters in our family—my father and uncles—all of whom were too old now for the hunt, though seeing those deer brought up the old stories about ones tracked years ago here, or in Maine, or Nova Scotia.

Our talk about the deer kept on, even when my father took sick. In the hospital he couldn't say much because his breathing was rapid and shallow. I sat by his bed—it was far into December by then—and his room, with its beeping monitors and hissing oxygen, was louder than anything outdoors. There were no real words, it felt late, but I was hoping he'd still want to know about the small things, so I told him I'd seen the deer that morning, that they were coming farther up into the orchard all the time. All he could do was blink his eyes, and I couldn't figure out if he knew what I was saying or if he had a question, but a little later, when I asked him if he wanted anything, he smiled as much as he could—I saw his cheek wrinkle—and whispered, "venison." One word that let through his dry wit, since he knew I wasn't much for hunting. One word that comforted me more than all the times he'd answered the usual questions we asked to make sure he still dwelled in time: Did he know where he was? Did he know the day? Or the questions he'd ask us when he could: What's the matter with me? Where's the blood coming from? Have you gone home?

A few mornings later, I was the first in the family to arrive at the hospital and I had to wait outside the room while the nurse finished her care. I knew something was wrong because she wasn't talking to him—always before I could hear the nurse asking my father how he felt, was he comfortable, telling him she was going to draw some blood. She beckoned me in this time and told me he had come down with pneumonia in the night. His hands were cold. It was louder in the room. They'd turned up the oxygen and had given him a larger mask through which to breathe. I could tell right away he was having trouble keeping up. When I said, "Hello," all he could do was raise his eyebrows. That was his last gesture to me in this life, and it's what I keep remembering, wishing for more, thinking of all his years of reserve and, in that last week, all his efforts to say the merest thing.

My mother, my brothers, my sister—all faces fell as they entered the room that morning. And no one dared step out for coffee or to make a phone call. We'd come a diligent way on a narrow trail since the gray early light of Christmas Eve day when I stood in the doorframe of my parents' house, and faced the road, listening in the still of the year for the ambulance to come. Now we gathered bewildered around his bed as his breathing grew quieter and quieter. He took his last breath, then his mouth closed. My mother whispered, "no,"

5

as the heart monitor slowed to a scribed outline like the low eroded hills, and each reading ended in a question mark.

When the doctor came he listened for my father's heart and his lungs, and then put a thumb to the lid of my father's blind eye and opened it, not knowing it had stopped gathering light years before, though my father always said he could still see the shadow of his own hand. Now, the coin for the journey.

Afterwards—in the days following—I sat at his desk and tried to carry on the workings of his home and farm: changing everything over to my mother's name alone, working out the payroll taxes, the quarterly taxes, all the January paperwork. I was half grateful for the dry figuring of accounts, of the farm year drawn to an abstraction of costs and balances. But such soldierly work couldn't keep grief at bay for long. As I backtracked over the check stubs, I saw how his handwriting had grown shakier down through the year. Like his voice, I'd start to think, becoming gravelly as his lungs weakened. Then I'd notice how quiet the house felt—and he was a quiet man. How did my mother stand it? How would she get through the days, the meals, the evenings? No answering words. Only months later beginning to understand: *never again.*

As I worked I'd uncover keepsakes of his in the drawers of the desk or tucked away among his ledgers and files. His original birth certificate, the death notices of his close friends who had gone before him, his own father's timepiece with its etched copper backing worn fine and the crystal clouded over—mute things that had lost the one who could best speak for them. From now on they'll only be partially understood, same as the stories I can no longer verify that were mostly his alone. "No one believes me," I remember him saying, "but I stood by the Bay of Fundy on the eve of the war and saw apples coming in on the tide. The bay was full of apples. The ships had dumped their cargoes to take on supplies for the war." That's all I know. And no matter how much, I want to know more.

Prayer cards and letters of sympathy came through the mail as news of his death traveled out of the valley. My aunts had been tearing obituaries out of the local papers and sending them to the relatives in Syracuse and Delaware. Friends of far friends wrote and called. I phoned my parents' closest friends in Florida—people I'd never called before—who knew something was wrong the moment they heard my voice. After their weak greeting, a questioning silence into which I poured, "I wanted to tell you my father passed away."

I know their true grief is beyond the formal, scripted sorrow that lands on his desk with every mail. I know my father would have understood their efforts to find words that come near. Near enough, OK, what we settle for while we tilt an ear to the winter air. I feel as if I've been listening—for what?—ever since the wake. It had started spitting snow, and those arriving to pay their respects, though they'd only walked from the parking lot to the door of the funeral home, seemed as if they'd made a real journey the way they stamped their boots and shook the snow from their scarves. They blew on their hands as they cleared their throats on comfortable sayings about the weather: "Sure is cold . . ." and "The roads are icing up." Then, the plush hallways and the floral sprays brought their voices down: "I can't believe it. I thought he'd live forever." Voices that had surrounded us all our lives

7

sounded graver than I'd ever known, murmuring, "Things just won't be the same," "I'm sorry," "Sorry for your troubles," "I had no idea. I saw him just a few days before Christmas and he seemed fine," "It'll be tough."

Eyes, then eye, that saw. Ears, then muffled ears, that heard. When I try to imagine afterwards, I keep coming back to how much my father belonged to this one place on earth. I can't imagine more than all he had in his keeping: three houses, forty cleared acres, a hundred of woodland, and a dozen in fruit trees. *Thou canst not follow me now, but thou shall follow me afterwards.* If *after* is a word that doesn't come near, if what's to come can't be imagined from this life, then why does his farm seem to mean all the more to me now, as I stand in the orchard when the moon is down and watch the comet passing?

His is a New England farm, and for all the stony soil, there's an intimate feel to the lay of the land with its small fields set off by chinked walls and the mixed woods beyond. My father's understanding of this place had accreted over eighty-five years, and at times I know he drove the wedge into wood with the resentment of the responsible son, at times with an effort born only of love. Over eighty-five years the original sound had swallowed its own echoes, and the most he could do was to tell me, "This is where I keep the receipts, this is where I keep the outstanding bills," as he opened the drawers in his office. Not much different from when he tried to teach me to prune the peaches: "This branch . . . here . . . see how the light will get through now?" as I stood puzzling it out alongside him.

So, with the snow falling outside, and the deer lunging through the deepening drifts, I am left to figure the farm from the notes on his desk, from the business cards he had scribbled across. I find a name—*Very Fine, Cal Jennings, Orchard Supply*—and work back from there. The world I'm responsible for is more complex and less patient than the one he was born into. Hospital bills from his last illness are waiting, the pension fund needs proof of his death. Over the phone I have to recite his Social Security number to prove I know him. I have to mail out his death certificate again and again—the form itself, with its raised stamp, is what they want, not the facts that his parents were born in Lebanon and that it was his heart and kidneys that gave out. Even when such work goes smoothly, I sometimes throw down the pen and ask the desk, the walls, and the ledgers why I couldn't have learned all this before.

And then a day comes when I have to erase his name from another account. First it was the checking account, then the Agway charge, and the Harris Seed charge. Sometimes it feels as if I'm erasing him everywhere until his name will remain only in his last place, on the hill, behind the white birch. I hate it, both the erasure and my realization that if we are going to go on I can't make the same decisions he would have made. I'm planning to spend more on repairs to the machinery than he ever would have agreed to. I'm thinking of selling a piece of far land as soon as the market's better.

"Who's going to be farming in this valley ten years from now? Who?" my father once asked. I could say nothing in the face of the long years he had put in. I realize I know little of the work it will be, even though it's not a great deal of land.

These acres he has left are almost nothing in comparison to the farms to the west, to farms in general. But it is ours, and one of the last here, and it feels huge to me.

In his safe, among the canceled bank books and the stock certificates, I found the original deed to the farm. In 1902 it had been a thirty-five-acre holding with worn implements and gradey cattle. All the scattered outbuildings are described in detail, and every boundary is fixed: *Thence northerly by said Herrick land as the fence now stands, to land now or formerly of Herbert Coburn, thence easterly by said Almon Richardson land as the fence now stands to the corner of a wall by said Almon Richardson land ... thence southerly ... thence westerly by the Black North Road to the point of beginning.*

The contents of the barns are listed, too: the hoes and shovels, the scythes and hammers, the Concord coach, the jump-seat wagon, two bay mares and their harnesses, five dairy cows and one milk pung, about thirty-five hens and all the chickens, one tip cart, and a blind horse. Plus feed for the blind horse. I swear, the worth of every nail is accounted for. For this my grandparents were so far mortgaged they had to cut down the pine grove to meet the payments. And now out of all that has been listed there, what has not been discarded or crumbled to a sifted heap hangs gathering an oily dust in the back of the carriage house or in the bins of the toolshed. The scythes have rusted to the nails they hang from, the leather collars for the horses have dried and cracked.

When all is said and done and we tally the contents of my father's estate, such things will no longer be counted among his worth. What brought us here and forward, the things he started with back in his boyhood where his allegiances began, will be smiled at indulgently and hung back up and considered as nothing alongside the larger things that have replaced them—the Case tractor, the gleaming red harrow, the corn planter. Stand at the door of the barn and breathe in the must of those early things. Listen for a voice—*hey bos, bos, bos*—calling the cows home. Feel an ache in the worked-out shoulders and cold creeping into the firelit rooms. How else could we have come this way since the April day when, according to the deed, my grandfather, who could hardly write his name in English, made his mark?

2

The Quality of Mercy

AFTER SYNTAX IS GONE, AND THE LITURGY, the maxims, the songs, even after no one can read anything of the old alphabet, and the names of things that remain are recognizable only to the few—after all, ragged bits of story still come down from the old country and are told in a new tongue: dry, sturdy, thin as the last weeds to be covered by a January snow. Sometimes those stories feel like tests when they're told. *Don't you remember ... Haven't you heard ...* how she was smuggled into this country under her mother's skirts, how they had to get him out after he'd killed that man in a fistfight, how they wanted to send her back because of the weeping in her eye ...

I imagine the stories my Lebanese grandparents carried with them had been at first as bulky as a peddler's pack stocked with lace and thread and stockings. My grandmother, not yet eighteen, traveled with her goods along the roads surrounding Olean, New York, and, as she exchanged lace and thread and her own handiwork for pennies, she glimpsed through each opened farmhouse door another life in the offing—the rush of warmth from stove heat, the smell of hard soap, of johnnycake and drying apples. And with each opened door, her pack lightened, and the stories shifted their place in her memory.

After Olean, Lawrence, Massachusetts. At the end of the nineteenth century it was the Immigrant City, the worsted and woolen capital of the world. For miles red brick textile mills lined the banks of the canals and the Merrimack River, and they contained so many looms and spindles that workers came to the city from Canada and all the countries of Europe and the Middle East to tend them. Within the central district you could hear forty-five—some say fifty or sixty—different languages and dialects spoken by dyers, cutters, spinners and weavers, by men who fixed the looms and rigged the warps, and women who felt along the yardage for slubs. Their children hauled coils of soft sliver and breathed in air that was white with cloth dust. Always cloth dust, falling constant as high mountain flurries.

The Italians settled near the commercial district, the Portuguese and Jewish neighborhoods were a little farther north and west. The Franco-Belgians found a place by the Merrimack above the dam, the Poles along the thin, sinewy Spicket River that wound through the north side of the city and eventually joined the Merrimack. The Syrians, as they were then known, settled several thousand strong on the slight rise blocks above the commercial district and the river—several thousand who'd walked through night dust storms and across mountain passes, and sailed the winter gray Atlantic to pass bewildered through ports of entry so as to keep shop, and sell wares, and take up unskilled jobs in the mills where they were among the lowest paid of all the workers. However far the journey, they continued to sing their Mass in Arabic, and their corner stores sold thyme, sesame paste, rose water, and the dried cherry kernels we call *mahleb* that flavor our Easter sweets.

For my grandparents, the life they'd glimpsed in the offing wasn't there among the familiar language or aroma of spices in the neighboring shops. "God knows how they ever got the money together," my father once said, for twenty acres of tillage on the south side, and an early nineteenth-century farmhouse and fifteen acres on the north side of a dirt road—sometimes known as the Black North Road—five miles west of Lawrence's tenement district and halfway to the city of Lowell.

A hundred years before they arrived in this country, a man named Moses Bailey had raised the first rough buildings on the property: a shed and a cottage he used as his shoe shop and living quarters, which in time became the central link in the long, curved spine of what we think of as a New England farm. Bailey's son extended the cluster of buildings eastward by raising a two-bay carriage house and a white clapboard cow barn topped with a windmill. Westward he added an ell for a summer kitchen, and southward from that ell he built a two-story-and-garret home. It is a dream of the solid and ordinary, the gable roof with its plain sloping sides, the serene rows of windows—two lights over two—without ornament, the two chimneys breaching the roofbeam. The eight fireplaces assured that even if the corners and attic remained cold enough to keep the summer harvest, there'd be a spot of warmth in every room.

If you were to slip off the leather latch of a Farmer's Diary from those years and turn the pages past the calendar, past the measure of length, the measure of surface, the measure of solidity, past the apothecary's weight and the diamond weight, the dry measures, the tests for death and the cure for cinders in the eye, you could read the concentrated words of those winter days: *Wednesday, January 4: Finished hauling in ice. Thursday, January 5: Got the sawdust back into the ice house. Tuesday, January 31: 6 below. Pump froze up. February 9: Zero. Sawing wood in the woodhouse. Cold windy day.... Samuel Knight died this noon. Jim went down to his sister's.... Mr. Knight's funeral.... Tough New England storm. Snow flying. Hard wind blow. Sawing wood and churning.*

By the time my grandparents bought the farm early in this century, the chain of buildings Moses Bailey had started a hundred years before was as long and rambling as it would ever be. In a 1901 photograph I can count six different roof heights, the most prominent being that of the broad-peaked house. By then its separate doors led to separate worlds. The daily one faced the work yard and the outbuildings, the place where they made their repairs in spring, where they rigged up the bay mares and loaded the milk wagon. The front door— dressed with an overhang—was the one place that allowed for shade, the one place to shelter a formal visitor. It faced the road to the cities.

With the land and house came much of the life of those who'd gone before, their tools and cattle, their hens and chickens, and whatever they could coax out of the wash and drift from the age of glaciers. My grandfather plowed the richest soils for the garden and the crop of hay; the indifferent, he used for pasture; the worst, let go to woods. The orchard spread across a droughty slope. Over time they came to judge for themselves the particular soils of the country—the sweet or sour, early or late. As they cleared stones and harvested potatoes and recorded their monthly payments to the bank, they would have been too intent on their work to notice that the last local map of agriculture was being drawn.

As I was going through my father's papers in the days after his death I came across what must have been that last map— the 1924 *Soil Survey of Middlesex County*. A booklet details the particular, elaborate name and best use of every soil to be found here, and the accompanying map lifts every inch of earth from its dun color and assigns it a rich, saturated one. The colors swirl and eddy—they remind me of Italian marbled paper—with fine distinctions and varying promises: the yellows of Hollis and the oranges of Sudbury loams, the pink of the Gloucester gravelly phase. The pale blue of Hinckley gravelly sandy loam: *derived largely from coarse glacial drift ... drainage, which is almost entirely internal, is usually excessive to the extent that crops suffer in dry seasons.... Crop yields are generally low. Hay cuts from one-half to three-fourths ton to the acre, depending on the season.... This land can be utilized for pasture, but it is not well suited to grass.* Merrimac gravelly sandy loam: *Nearly all the vegetables grown for market in this county are found on this soil, but asparagus is the only one grown on a large acreage. A few farmers make a specialty of chickens. Hay yields range from 1 to 1 1/2 tons to the acre on the best-farmed land.... The soil is easy to cultivate. It is plowed 8 or 9 inches deep and can be brought into good tilth without difficulty.* Coloma sandy loam, gravelly phase: *differs from the typical soil in having a larger proportion of stones and gravel on the surface and throughout the soil.... It can be utilized for pasture land, but it furnishes only indifferent grazing. The rougher areas should be left in forest or should be reforested to white pine.*

The soft hills to our south are marked as drifts of Hinckley loamy sand—*a small acreage is in pasture, a still smaller area is in mowing*—and Gloucester stony loams. The soil of the river bank beyond those hills isn't deposited in pockets like most other county soils but has washed and settled in narrow bands along both sides of the watercourse—thin stretches, influenced by the drenchings and drainings of mountain water: *brown mellow fine sandy loam ... not inundated with every overflow but covered by the spring freshets.... The land is easily plowed and cultivated, coming readily into good tilth. ... The overflow in spring is depended on in measure to keep up fertility.* This map is the only local one I've seen where the Merrimack's presence is so slight—really it's almost lost amid the colors of over forty soil types, just a faint blue bend cutting through the reds and greens and oranges in its eastward turn to the sea, as if to suggest we were once a people defined by something other than the river and the red brick cities that line the drops along its lower course.

Any map is bounded by scope and hand and eye, by the particulars of the world it describes. I don't think the soils of Middlesex County will ever again be so painstakingly described and drawn. Contemporary soil maps consist of data imposed on aerial photographs. Colorless, perfunctory, stiff with information alone, the new maps chart moist bulk density and the shrink-swell potential of soils with exactitude, but the grain of the old language with its good tilth and its indifferent pasture is gone, just as hames and traces and milk pungs are gone from our conversations.

*

Our farm is no longer a self-regarding world. The barn and the silo have been lost to wind and rain, and with them, the long protective curve of buildings around the east yard that shielded daily life. The house stands more prominent than the remaining farm buildings, and more solitary. A side porch makes it less plain; the maples shading the lawn, less blazed upon by the summer sun. Crocus, then iris, then roses, until the rust chrysanthemums bloom in mid-October.

Moses Bailey's original cottage survives to this day in its place between the house and the carriage house, and we continue to use it as a storage room and toolshed. Its clean white clapboard exterior blends in with the line of remaining buildings. Walk inside though, and you feel the length of its days. Its windows are blocked from full sun by two cedars so that, even at noontime, it's a pool of cool shadows. The boards of the interior walls are rough-sawn, not once sanded or painted in all their years. The smell of must. On the rafters a hundred nails have been sunk for a hundred hooks—lanterns, oilcans, chains. Look how everything is becoming the same color. The bins full of bolts and screws, the anvil and ax, the hammers, spades, and hoes, even the white pine floor and the hardwood rafters, the paper on crates and the notices pinned to the walls—all the same brown as acorns and fallen oaks.

If the interior of the farmhouse—its fireplaces blocked off, old papers piled in the bread ovens, half the clocks stopped— also feels like twilight, to think of it only as it is now is to miss much of the story, which continues to waken and glimmer in the eyes of those who lived there, in the eyes of one of my uncles remembering seventy years back, and the May evenings he read to his mother as she darned socks and knitted sweaters. She'd want to hear the stories he was learning at college—

Shakespeare was her favorite—so over and over again he read her *The Merchant of Venice.* By the late acts the sun had faded back from the dining-room table and was retreating from the orchard, his dutiful voice was growing tired. Her knitting needles clicked: *The quality of mercy is not strain'd, it droppeth as the gentle rain from heaven upon the place beneath; it is twice bless'd....*

The story never stopped on the last page. Days, months later he'd hear her tell a clear, clean version to his sisters as they made bread or pies or stuffed grape leaves. A version indiscernible in tenor from the stories she'd sometimes tell that she'd heard back in the dry hills of her own childhood. She'd begin: *There was an Italian ...,* and when she wanted to pause for emphasis or to keep up the suspense, she spent an extra moment pushing the silky dough away with the palm of her hand, then drawing it towards her again.

3

Armistice Day

AS MY FATHER'S EYES, HEARING, AND KNEES failed ever more certainly, his inner world seemed to grow stronger. In his last year he was steeped in remembrances of his childhood, sometimes of the smallest things—squirting milk from a cow's udder into the cat's mouth as he did the morning chores, or picking blueberries with his grandfather, or planting potatoes in the back field. Other times he remembered epidemics and storms, and the way war made its inroads. Or small events that shook their world—the farm was a remote place then and it didn't take much for something, a wild beehive or a flooded brook, to be talked about for weeks and remembered long into the century.

In part, hearing those stories helped me to feel closer to him in the years since I'd come back to live on the farm. Certainly when I listened to him remember—relaxed in his worn leather chair, his voice unrushed—he was no longer the remote, capable, eternally working figure he'd been in my childhood. Without question back then we were over forty years apart, and now in his late years it was as if these moments of recollection allowed for a breach in the strict chronology of time.

Still, that sense of nearness was now durable, now fleeting. As his past grew more vivid, he also became more placid about letting go of the here and now, about the fate of the farm whatever it may be, as if he knew it was already out of his hands. In those moments I felt helplessly far from him, and almost betrayed, what with me dreaming of a constant future. And in his final months, when there was no stopping the reel of stories, as he began calling up the past all the time, the more he remembered, the more he appeared to be on a rise looking back on a complete, clear life. I knew it signaled his end, and began to feel afraid. Some days, when he started in, all I wanted was air.

Now that he's gone those accreted stories hardly seem enough—a few marks carved by a burin is all—and I find myself trying to make up the world around them. I study them for clues not only to his life, but to the life of those before him. My grandparents spoke other tongues—Arabic on my father's side, Italian on my mother's—and our family doesn't have much of a written past. There are no boxes of letters, no journals wrapped in burlap, not even a Farmer's Diary. My oldest aunt kept notes in her careful hand of all the family names and addresses, marriages, deaths, and children. Beyond that the family record is kept in documents— mortgages, deeds, and citizenship papers. *Be it remembered ... the said applicant having made such declaration and renunciation and taken such oaths.... or, Know all men by these presents....* Tucked in drawers or locked in a steel safe fitted into one of the old fireplaces, such documents are what we have to assure ourselves *they* were back there living their lives.

I know the details of a few often-repeated stories—not

many—by heart. Though they may seem random, they hold together what I have like the galvanized nails my father used to repair his apple boxes. The original nails have rusted and bled into the wood, but the ones he himself struck gleam out of the time-darkened pine. Here in its modest blue-white luster is Armistice Day 1918. He laughed to remember it: "That afternoon we must have sung *Marching Through Georgia* dozens of times."

Their schoolroom smelled of ink and chalk and musty readers. In autumn they trailed in sodden leaves, in spring their boots reeked of skunk cabbage. Their cheeks glistened in the falling of a small rain. In winter the room could be smoky and the stove sometimes ran too hot; come late spring a glare spread across the wooden desks. On the walls hung oak-framed gray prints of George Washington and Abraham Lincoln and a map of the world with its old borders drawn in black. White rings stained the sills where jars of frogs' eggs had ranged in spring. The flawed window glass sent tremors through the pines and a steely November sky. A tongue curled over an upper lip, a furrow crossed a translucent blue-veined brow as their hands made ghost strokes above their papers before they drew the first mark.

They were learning the Palmer method of penmanship, and it accompanied them all their lives. I still see old men signing checks at the bank, and they circle the air with diagonal O's to get the right slant and set before setting down their signature as if even their names were thought out and practiced before being written. For my father and his sisters and brothers that motion was more than effort and caution, since each pen stroke brought them a little further from their parents' alphabet, even as it granted them new letters fit for their world.

The eleventh day of the eleventh month of 1918 was a quiet, usual morning. Most still traveled the roads by foot and horse and wagon, so all raised their heads from their work when the sound of an approaching engine became audible, and they grew even more attentive when it idled down. Hastening footsteps, and then the regional school superintendent threw the door open while announcing, "Armistice has been signed! Armistice has been signed! Spread the word!"

"I didn't even know what the word *armistice* meant," my father said. For the Second World War there'd be three stars in the window of the farmhouse, and each brother would know differing wars within that war: the one who'd read Shakespeare was a colonel in the Pacific and has countless stories to tell; another, a soldier in France, has never, as far as I know, said a thing. But in 1918 my father was barely eight, and none in his family had gone over, so his memory of the time is that of a child's, no harsher than a feather falling across his good eye. "What did we know of the war? My mother knit scarves and sweaters at night. We picked out peach pits from the chicken feed. We had no white sugar."

To spread the word their teacher lined them up, the youngest in front, the oldest holding the flag at the rear, and marched them north down Salem Road, then west on Pelham Road. "These were great distances we're talking about . . ." Small steps on an uneven rutted way:

> *Bring the good old bugle, boys, we'll sing another song,*
> *Sing it with a spirit that will start the world along,*
> *Sing it as we used to sing it fifty thousand strong,*
> *While we were marching through Georgia.*

All the holdings they paraded past were carved out of the same world—a tie-up in the barn, a farmhouse facing south so the yard would be out of the bitter wind and early to warm up in spring, a good place for the first work of the new season. In seeing the way those old houses sit in place I'm tempted to see the same lives in each—there were more than four thousand farms in this county and half the land was under cultivation. But there were many ways of division. As the milk inspectors looked over the farms that supplied Lawrence with milk, they saw a difference, and divided the holdings into the kept and unkempt: *noticeable lack of equipment and method at this farm,* or, *up to date farm . . . common farm buildings having ample means of light for the cows,* or, *insufficient light; no milk room; illustration of an old and cluttered farm,* or, *run by men of foreign birth who have no one to keep house for them . . .*

White pine on the terraces, swamp maple in the lowlands.

> *Hurrah! Hurrah! We bring the jubilee!*
> *Hurrah! Hurrah! the flag that makes you free!*
> *So we sang the chorus from Atlanta to the sea,*
> *While we were marching through Georgia.*

He remembers how deserted the road seemed. Mid-afternoon. The chestnut mare at Wyatt's lifted her head from the feed and turned towards them. Mrs. Timson was so far back they couldn't read her expression but saw a wave of her hand. No one home at the Kennedy farm, or Baileys', Mansur. Only the hired man at the Stewarts' walked towards the road and called out, "So, the Kaiser quit?"

"The Kaiser quit," their teacher answered and marched on past more spare yards containing carts and plows, stovewood cut and partially stacked next to a stump with an ax cocked on it. The windmill fluttered in a diminishing wind. A porch hadn't yet been built and the maple planted to mark the first birth was still a sapling, so nothing softened the frame of the white clapboard house trimmed in white. Their hope was that it would soften with time—that a branch of the maple would shelter the parlor from the July sun, and the lilac would scent the second-story bedrooms. But then it was full of effort, and who would believe the world could come to them on this road, dust-choked in summer, the low places impassable in mud time?

The town—fewer than five thousand then—had sent nearly two hundred young men to serve in the infantry, artillery, batteries, in the navy, the aviation corps. 319th Regt. Field Artillery, Battery F. They were engaged at Chemin Des Dames, Seichprey-Xivray, the Argonne Meuse Forest, St. Mihiel, Chateau Thierry. They'd left a world that, if noted at all, was noted in the same clasped leather book that listed the phases of the moon and the position of the morning stars. And noted in a meted-out hand: *July 3: Mowed the new orchard; July 4: Went down to the Grange for dinner; July 5: Mowed with the horses, got in two loads; July 9: A good rain this afternoon; July 10: Good hay day, got in three loads. . . . Got in four loads.*

Some soldiers wrote long chronicles of the war in France, as if the strangeness of what they'd seen had given them a new eloquence: *As we rode along in the train we noticed old trenches, barbed wire . . . we could hear guns booming in the distance. . . . On that afternoon we went to a nearby ruined village, where to test our gas masks, we put them on and went into a cave where there was gas. . . . We noticed orchards everywhere where the trees had been sawed a few feet from the ground and toppled over. The churches and gravestones had been smashed to dust.*

The schoolchildren marched past all that the men would return to, the grade herds, the milk houses, past barbed wire over stone walls, and then turned and marched back past the schoolhouse to the main road. By then, lamps were lit in the kitchens, herds in narrow file were making their way back to the barns. Weak bells tinkled in the late afternoon. On the uneven road, the teacher didn't notice the children's voices were growing fainter. *A grass widow,* is what my father heard people call her, though at the time he couldn't have understood what was meant by the term. In the winter months she buried heated bricks at the foot of her bed for warmth. She broke the skin of ice that had formed on the water in her china washbasin and slipped her cupped hands in. At the junction of the main road she stopped singing, and for the first time she gathered how half-hearted the voices were behind her. A ragged line of pink in the west, pink on the eastern hills. The moon growing solid as the sky sloped towards evening. She turned towards them to find the flag had been passed forward and the oldest children, who had taken up the rear, had deserted. They had been sneaking off one after another, escaping through the fields and woods, their clothes snagging on damask rose vines along the walls, black alders whipping at their eyes. They gulped the damp woods air, their boots were caked with mud and duff; their faces, flush with their antics. What was left of her parade was four children under eleven carrying the song. Seeing how far the daylight had gone, she dismissed them.

*

26

It's likely word spread faster from Paris, France, to Lawrence than it had from farm to farm. In the city the fire horns
had sounded off at three in the morning to announce the end
of the war, and by noon there was an extra edition of the paper
outlining the terms of armistice. The five o'clock edition reported Germany was in the hands of revolutionists. The war
machine was already dismantling: all outstanding draft calls
were canceled, overtime and Sunday war work orders for the
mills were stopped. Even so, the call for liberty bonds continued, as did the three-column ads for Arrowsmith artificial
limbs. Retail grocers were asked to call at City Hall to receive
sugar registry cards. Private McKeown had been killed in
France. *Born in Ireland twenty-eight years ago [he] came
here when he was eight years old. At the time of his enlist-
ment he was a wool sorter in the Washington mills and is well
known in the city. Private McKeown has one brother who
has been discharged from the Canadian army after being
badly gassed. Another brother, Peter, is a member of Battery
D 45th Field Artillery in France.*

On November 12 there was a long, large Victory parade in
the city, which my grandfather took my father to see. Mill
workers stood measured paces apart and donned matching
hats and aprons and marched along with schoolchildren and
veterans and Red Cross workers past the shops and banks of
the wide commercial streets. What he remembers of that day
is not the parade but the crowds back in the side streets, where
the triple-decker porches sagged, where the laundry hanging
across the alleyways stiffened in the cold late fall winds, back
where the tenements were so close together that the rent collector could save himself three flights of stairs by reaching
across the alley from one kitchen window to the next to collect

what was due him, and where the official songs of the parade faded into songs of countless languages, and voices talking and calling.

The war—and its end—had separated many of the immigrants even further from their birthplaces, further from the hopes they'd raised with each glass of wine. A common toast among them: *May your return home be soon.* Which was answered with: *In your company.* After four years some of their old villages were heaps of rubble, some a muddy field of the dead. When my father's parents immigrated, their village near Xahle had been part of Greater Syria under the rule of the Ottoman Empire—my father's birth certificate says his parents were born in Syria. Following the First World War, half the population of their village and its surrounding countryside starved or died of disease. The country of my grandparents' birth came under French rule, then years later became the independent country of Lebanon; it's listed as such on my father's death certificate, as if a ghost journey had been made through colonial determinations, through independence and bitter civil war. In the eyes of the world Lebanon has made a passage from an obscure Middle Eastern country to one whose daily casualties make international headlines; and there, between my father's birth and his death, roams what might have been had my grandparents never put their lives in the hands of steamship agents and translators.

As it was, the loved ones the Lawrence mill workers left behind had seen what they themselves had only heard of. In the alleyways of Lawrence, in a confusion of languages, the crowds burned the Kaiser in effigy—my father remembers seeing that—they hit him in effigy. Eight million had died. The dove, if she comes, will have to rest her breast on the rough road and peck at stones.

The school has been razed, the road paved. The houses that have been built on old fields are oriented to the roads and to the life of the towns and cities. There isn't any need to have a warm east-facing yard for the spring repairs. No significant time is told by almanacs and moons. I have in my house the oak frame from the portrait of George Washington that once hung on the wall of the one-room school. It now frames a watercolor of the farm, which had first hung in my father's office. He told me a woman had come out one day and asked permission to set up her easel in one of the fields, and at the end of the day she gave my father the painting because he had brought her a glass of beer earlier that afternoon.

He used to say she got a good portion of it right: the boards missing on the barn, which has since blown down, and the tilt of the silo, gone too. The tree she painted to the right of the barn by the stone wall was never there, but he didn't have a problem with that. The woman who'd spent that afternoon looking at the side of the barn and house, who'd thinned her colors and dipped her brush into spring water must have wanted something to balance the picture.

4

Milk

"ALL YOU COULD SMELL WAS COWS," AND HE tamped his ash cane on the living room floor as he named down the farms: "Bragdon had thirty cows, Dooley must have had twenty or so. Stevens, he had a small herd . . . Cox, Clough . . ." Neighbors whose places were nearly like his own family's—cattle fed on mash and scraps, and grass in summer. The morning's yield cooled in metal jugs set in stone rooms, in springs, and in wellhouses before it was sold to the mill workers in Lawrence.

In the early years of the city, a farmer would bring his own supply to the central district. He'd load his cans on the back of his wagon and cover them with damp blankets to keep out the dust. When he reached the tenements, he'd pull up halfway down a street and the women would come down the outside stairwells carrying tin pitchers, enamel basins, bowls, mason jars, anything that would hold their day's supply of milk. Five cents a quart, three cents a pint—the first customers got all the cream—until his ladle scraped the bottom of a can and he poured the last blue milk into a mason jar.

By 1910 the three-hundred-acre central district contained

over thirty thousand people, and one man ladling out milk to a waiting cluster of women proved too small and singular an act to sustain the growing population. Farms farther and farther away began shipping milk in until the Lawrence milkshed extended farther than the Merrimack River watershed—to northern Maine, to the Canadian border of Vermont. Supplies came down in bulk by rail, and plants near the city bottled and distributed the milk.

The nearby farmers, too, began consolidating their production. Bottlers on the outskirts of the city would collect the milk from area farms, process it, then make door-to-door deliveries. In the predawn hours boys ran up the tenement steps, set down full quarts at every threshold, and retrieved the empty ones. You could hear the glass chime when the bottles jostled against each other. The cream froze in winter and forced off the paper plug. Milk set down in the dark at every door—that custom of delivery lived well into the 1960s—I remember it too—and it's the way I always imagine milk: frosty, clean in its clear bottle. Think of all the kind words and phrases that come from it: *milky, milk glass, milk run, milk tooth...*

Milk epidemic. I remember my father saying, "Dr. Batal tells me the undertakers always had a dozen child's coffins on hand—it was the milk." It was also the water, and the raw sewage, and the lack of medical attention. But scarlet fever, typhoid, diphtheria, septic sore throat, dysentery could be spread through milk, and because the supply had started to come from a greater distance, and the plants combined the supply from one small farm with all the other milk of the day, of several milkings, it meant the yield from one herd could find its way into countless households, and you could no longer trace a ladle of it back to its source.

As it was, families in the central city were so squeezed in there was little room for health: their long hours at work, the bad air, the cramped conditions, breakfasts of bread soaked in coffee. For those surveying the state of public health in Lawrence in 1910, the milk supply was as much of a concern as the water supply and sewage and garbage disposal. They recommended tighter inspections of dairies and farms, pasteurization of all milk, and a grading system based on cleanliness. In a world once judged by the cream line, the rule would soon be: the cleaner the milk, the higher the price. Certified Milk, Inspected Milk Heated, Market Milk Heated . . .

Inspectors visited every local farm to check one man's holding against all the others, and to an ideal. *Do you wash your hands before milking?* they asked. *Do you wash the udders? Do you cool the milk immediately after milking each cow? How much ice do you have on hand in summer? When was the herd last tested with tuberculin?* They took the temperature of the well water and checked the milk for impurities. They examined the sturdiness of the barn and the cleanliness of the bedding; suggested separate milk rooms; told the farmers their jugs should have narrower openings to lessen the chances for contamination. Their stables should be as light as the kitchen.

A cold eye on dust and rain in an open pail, rough boards, a cluttered yard. Of course they found cause for concern: a live frog in a milk can, bottles washed in a galvanized tub out in the open, manure piled against the barn windows. To the long-established farmers, it must have seemed as if their very lives were being questioned. Men standing in where their fathers had, working as their fathers had, coming to understand they couldn't teach their children all they'd need to know. Children who smelled of hay and dung and souring milk as they studied their times tables and Whittier's poems in the one-room school on the back road.

The Civil War, the industrial age, the opening of the West, and the played-out soil had already thinned the rural families throughout New England. The rougher fields had gone to woods, and barns had collapsed in on themselves. What survived? Lilacs, the stone walls, the cellar holes, the metal and glass dumped in the dry well. Even with all those lost farms, what must have seemed a paucity then looks like an abundance now. When I spread out the 1911 map of the Lawrence milk supply, I can count over one hundred and fifty holdings within a six-mile radius of the city: *Connelly, 200 quarts; Griffen, 80 quarts; Williams, 450; Boornazian, 130.*

To a world already in the midst of change Lawrence, with its short, dense history, brought even more changes to the surrounding farmlands. Coburn, Cox, Clough—names that had settled the valley—half at least would soon disappear from the farming maps; in their place, the names of Greeks, Armenians, Italians, Poles. No one, not the city planners, not the old farmers, not the immigrants themselves would have imagined that as the settlers moved on to other opportunities, or simply faded out, immigrants would move out of the city to take up farming in unfamiliar soil.

Five hundred dollars bought my grandparents their thirty-five acres and house and barn and herd, and that's more or less what they left to their nine children sixty years later. *Know all men by these presents,* my grandfather's Last Will and Testament begins, *that I, Kalil Brox otherwise known as Charles Brox, Kilil Brox, Kelle Brox, and Kelil Brox* . . . To document his life, he had to include all the official spellings of his Arabic name. The farm hardly appeared different from others on the road: trodden dirt in the barnyard, the brief bloom of the peonies. Woodsmoke rising all winter long; and in summer, the sound of a man coaxing a workhorse, or the scythe cutting the dry June grass. The smell of hay and manure. Rather than journey to the Arabic church in Lawrence, my father and his brothers and sisters went to Sunday school at the Methodist church next door. They brought their lunches to the neighborhood box parties and leaned over their primers in the kerosene light at night.

When city relatives came to the farm for visits—the children to spend time in some good air, the adults to pick grape leaves or apples—they walked out from Lawrence on foot early in the day, singing Syrian songs for all five miles, and once here they'd eat under the remaining white pines: roasted lamb, red pistachios, stuffed eggplants, and figs. All day long the closest neighbor walked back and forth along his property line, making sure not one of those visitors stepped over onto his land. Strangers here; and the children, strangers here and in the city. After he graduated from the one-room school, my father took the trolley to Lawrence to go to high school, where a child who had never milked a cow in his life, who hunted the railroad tracks for scrap coal and brought lunch to his parents in the mill, who likely would go on to work in the mill himself after school was finished, a child smelling of cabbage, or of scrap coal, or of kerosene, found the difference and split it. He said with contempt and out of the side of his mouth, "You smell like a barn."

I can't find any record of a milk epidemic having occurred in the valley. There needn't have been anything so drastic for milk to become a losing proposition here. Competition from larger farms in the Midwest, and other possibilities for lives and land took care of that. The livestock books on the shelf in my father's office haven't been opened for years. In order to keep the farm going he turned to growing vegetables for the Lawrence market, for Lowell, sometimes Boston. He loved growing things—in his last summers his whole heart seemed to be in his corn and tomatoes and apples—and I have never much pictured him around livestock, though he says he was a long time in giving it up and kept a couple of cows for years after he'd sold the bulk of the herd.

"Just for the family," he would have said. When the cows freshened, his mother and sisters wouldn't know what to do with all the milk. They were always making *laban*, tart and cold, close to what we call yoghurt now, a vestige brought forward from the desert life, where fermentation kept milk from spoiling. You start a new batch with a remnant from the old, and let it thicken in a covered bowl in the warmest spot in the kitchen. One batch would be mild and the next would make you wince with its tartness. Sometimes it was beaten or thinned so you could drink it. For a hot day, laban with cucumbers and mint; in winter, laban with raspberry jam spooned in contemplation by the kitchen window.

And palm-sized crumbly cakes of fresh Syrian cheese, they

made that too. They'd tie the curd in thin muslin and let it drain into an enamel bowl. On the kitchen counter, in the still of the afternoons, all through the night as the household slept, whey dripped off the cloth—first, resonant on the bowl's hard surface, then dripping more softly into itself, and slowing as the curd compacted. Cheese eaten with olives or wrapped in Syrian bread, crumbled between a thumb and forefinger, or sliced neat with a steel blade. White as the high, far moon. We grew up on it: tangy, salty, dry on the tongue.

5

Last Look

PHOTOGRAPHS—THE OLD ONES—AS BROWN AS barn light. I have several sitting on the table in my bay window, and when I catch a glimpse of them, I settle into a mild contentment, since my parents in them, in the wedding photo, in the antic day at the beach, are nearly unknown to me. So young, for one thing, dressed in the fashions of their time, the vintage cars shining behind them. They feel as far from me as the washed pen lines of old plats are from the current maps of this farm. When I look at them it doesn't seem I've lost the people in them to death or age. Not nearly the sorrow I feel when I look at later pictures, say, of my father in his seventies. The one I keep at the window is in full color. He's standing in the eggplant, snips in hand, smiling easily at the photographer: a picture of the father that I knew, in the shape of the daily life he lived, and I can't quite believe he is no longer here.

It's hard for me to remember anymore when he wasn't slow to get out of his truck—arthritis in his knees. His slowness gave him an air of deliberation as he considered the shapes of the apple trees and weighed which branches to prune. Arthritis in his shoulders, too, and he'd lift the saw in obvious pain, though his cuts were always sure. A few draws of the saw and the apple branch would drop to the grass. He'd work from the bottom to the top of each tree, pruning a few trees, and then driving on down the orchard with his truck door ajar. It would be one of the warmer mornings of late February or early March, and it's likely there was snow in the woods.

In his last years Felix, his oldest, most reliable worker, came back early to help him with the trees. Felix speaks mostly Spanish—he's from Puerto Rico—mixed with a little broken English, and I think if the two of them could have communicated better, my father might have taught him how to prune. As it was, the two of them worked at my father's pace, though it was obvious Felix could have worked much faster on his own; he always walked a little ahead, then waited, arms at his sides, until my father showed him which cuts to make. For the high cuts he pointed with his ash cane, which he'd bought years back at a cattle exposition—all the dairy farmers carried one to hook around the neck of a calf, drawing the face close for a better look at its eyes and teeth. The cane outlasted all the herds here, and my father used it to point out what needed to be done or to help himself down the stairs or to poke at a smoldering log. Some days he simply leaned against his truck and tamped the earth with it.

Touch-up prunings are what the orchard had gotten in those years, so there were shocks of watersprouts atop some of the older trees, crowns too thick with branches, and branches crossing one another. Its mild neglect settled in and became part of our lives, maybe like a little drinking or my mother tossing off the doctor's warnings by saying, "I'm fine, I just

have a bit of sugar in my blood is all." Even so, the trees stood
sturdy in our winter land. Their basic shape had been set long
ago by their early prunings, so the tiers turning off the central
leaders have a hard-earned grace about them, and the wide
crotches are full of strength. In winter they'd stand up to ice
storms and the nor'easters, and we stopped thinking of anything radical changing. Outside, a fine dry January snow falling on those turned limbs; within, my father studying his
Wall Street Journal in the easy chair, my mother biding time
in the kitchen, the layers of glass shutting out the small notes
of the chickadees.

And so they stayed until stirred one January by a phone call
from someone offering to prune the orchards. I imagine the
man who called drove the back roads of Middlesex and
Worcester counties looking for old farmers and old orchards.
Here the land values are so high there isn't much of a way to
have your own farm anymore unless you were born to it, and
those who were not have to find their place among established
family holdings. There are large places that need managers
and small places where an old farmer has no one to take over
or is having trouble with his children.

What is it about our farm that signaled a way in? A local
rumor maybe, or the watersprouts on the trees, or he might
have noticed how the orchard had gone unmown. High bur-
nished grasses he'd see, since the months had been dry. The
afternoon thunderstorms all veered to our north or south or
petered out in the blue hills of Worcester County. Every
afternoon signs of a storm would build and then fail. The
brown grasses—nearly the same color as the hide of a deer—
were shot through with purple vetch and white yarrow. I re-

member staring at those colors for a moment and not wanting it otherwise, it seemed so beautiful, even though I knew it wasn't practical for picking the crop or getting the trucks through, and how easily it could be sparked by fire.

"You can start on the new trees," my father told the man, "and we'll see." If he hesitated in his decision, it didn't show in his voice. Strange for me to hear. He had always loved best that early quiet work of pruning, the chance to start up again in spring, and I just didn't think he'd pass it on so easily. For my mother and me, once we got used to the idea, those were light days for us. Light beyond reason really. The thought of the pruner animated our talk. My mother's voice nearly sang as she recited where he had worked before: "In the Nashoba Valley, for Hanson, for Dawes." He had gone to Stockbridge, he had a license to spray. And my mother's mind and mine started running the same. We imagined how he could maybe head the picking crew as well. It seemed as if it were a move for the future instead of just getting through seasons. My father was more cautious: "He talks good. We'll have to see how he works out."

The man began the pruning on a cold March day. Frost in the shadows, the crocuses just breaking ground. Two trucks made their way down into the orchard; the two of them talked for a while at the first tree, and then the man got right to work. He hung his loppers over a low branch and folded a saw into his back pocket. His shears fit in a holster by his side. Only the pole, which he kept in his truck, was out of easy reach. He started right at a large branch on the first row of Cortlands, walked around the tree and made his cuts, then

walked straight to the next one and began again. I thought for
sure my father would shadow him for much of the first morning, but after a few trees he drove off.

The history of the trees that I'd heard piecemeal through
the years—how the orchard had been planted in an old pasture which had once been the white pine woods my grandfather logged to pay off the mortgage, or how a new orchard
blew down in the '38 hurricane and they'd staked the trees
back up with downed wires—none of it did he need to know
to do his job. What he had to know he could glean from what
was right in front of him in the turn of a branch, in the health
of the wood, in the cuts that had gone before. It may not have
been exactly how my father would have pruned the trees, but
there wasn't any arguing with his work. "He seems do be doing a good job," I said after the first day. "Well, those young
trees are easy," my father replied. I could see him setting his
jaw. A silence. And then he relented: "He knows what he's
doing."

The man arrived reliably in the early mornings, pruning to
his own ideal, probably thinking ahead to next year, saying to
himself he'd have an easier time of it then. He tended to prune
more severely than my father ever had. Where he cut the
larger limbs the honey-colored wood stood out against a gray
land. Familiar small branchings were gone. My eyes had to
adjust to a little more sky.

He'd leave his truck door open, the radio going, and the
noise made me a little cranky, but I never felt it was my place
to say anything. Felix went up and down the rows in the afternoon gathering the cuts into piles—more pruned wood than
I ever remembered in tangled heaps on the winter-matted

grass. They burned the piles one still day under a damp, leaden sky. A low flame was the color in the land. Brush fires have always been part of the early spring here—all smudge—and I cracked the window open so I could sleep to the smell the way I like to sleep to rain after the long dry spells.

6

At Sea

MONTHS AFTER EVERYTHING I WAS DRIVING headstrong into Boston—as abstracted as everyone else on the road—when out of the corner of my eye I saw an ambulance in silent alarm moving steadily through the rush hour traffic, and all my hasty thoughts stopped. I had to wince back tears as I remembered trying to stay calm when the medic told me not to rush as I followed the ambulance into Lowell.

That late December day there'd been patchy snow on the ground and the beginnings of a still gray winter dawn as I ran across the orchard to my parents' house. It seemed to take forever before the sirens cut into the morning. Then all at once five husky men—four EMTs and a policeman—tossed aside the chairs in the dining room so the gurney could get through, then stood around the bedposts in my parents' room where my father lay in pain. They'd brought in the cold dawn air. They'd tracked in melting snow.

The policeman turned to me and spoke in awkward apology: "Someone has to come for all the 911's—in case there's anything. But there's nothing like that here. Sorry. Jeez, it's been a bad night." And as he started to tell me about how some old man who lived on Hildreth Street had fallen out of bed, I tried to hear around him so I could discern what the medics were asking my father: "When did it start?" "Can you describe the pain?" "Can you get yourself up?" I was too afraid to enter the bedroom or to ask questions myself, so I stood in the entranceway overhearing what I could. One medic whispered to another: "He's extremely, extremely critical."

What do the dying see? A resolving flare of human love? Does a milky eye clear for the last time? From the little I know now, I think they must see what they always have, are true to their natures at the end—those of earth, tied to the earth. My father, who had always been practical, when given his last choice weakly told the EMTs to take him to the hospital in Lowell rather than Lawrence because, as he later explained, the winter roads were better maintained along that route, and we'd have an easier time getting back and forth if he was in for a long stay.

And it was a straight way there past the house he'd been born in, the orchards he'd planted, and up the hill that had once mired horses in spring in the time when the route was known as the Black North Road, which you can find on maps hundreds of years back, before our family's knowledge of this country, back past the oxen teams and wheel tracks to a footpath crossing the wilderness north of the Merrimack. Now it was a clear gray paved road for a small entourage just under the speed limit: a squad car, an empty rescue truck followed by the ambulance carrying my father—my mother sat up front with the driver—and me following last.

No other traffic that winter Sunday morning, so no siren, and only the merest slowing at intersections. The deliberateness of the ride was a strange foolish comfort as I told myself *it mustn't be too much of an emergency,* even as I knew for sure his kidneys were so weak he could not possibly survive a problem with his heart, and this was the closest he'd have to a last look at where he'd lived his life as we passed the neighbors, the town offices, the Grange hall, passed all the good will and any grudges and misjudgments, the red emergency lights sweeping across everything like a lighthouse beacon falling back across those sleeping in an innocent mist among low coastal hills who, since they are not the ones caught in a fogbound open sea, sleep unawares. Whoever we'd become in those hours, we were different from those on dry land.

Once in Lowell we skirted the river and its bridges and passed the brick mills and Pawtucket Falls where tawny winter water poured over the boards onto icy rocks at the bottom. Then we turned away from the river road, and the ambulance docked at the emergency entrance to The General.

The intensive care unit there is a circle of rooms around the nurses' station. The waiting area is an outer circle embracing the patients' rooms. You can walk around and around through the day and see the same groups of families camped in that outer circle—the ICU has no restrictions on visiting hours: exhausted men and women who'd come from their shifts, smelling of oil or of ink; old women sitting straight-backed, their eyes closed with strain, or maybe prayer; children sleeping at their parents' feet; spent coffee cups and Coke cans and snack wrappers scattered about. The ones who've just arrived hardly leave at all. Those there long enough might start thinking about spotting one another, coaxing one another to go home for some rest: *Come on, you have to keep your strength up* . . . You never think it could be so plain and small, but there it is: the best hope in that place is a long haul.

For nearly a week we were one family of the eleven waiting there in that circular hall, talking with several surrounding families, comparing progress or the lack of it, reading the slightest movement of a hand or the strength of a sigh for a sign. It seemed we were all on the same journey—odd comfort—and when my father turned quickly, and one afternoon six days after being admitted, his fire drowned in its own ash, we were set adrift on our own small raft again. How strange it was to have lived day and night for a week with those people, and now to hug them one last time and leave them forever to their own fates. I knew that by evening my father's bed would be filled by another.

7

What Is Kept

OF THE ARABIC MY GRANDPARENTS SPOKE, even my father knew next to nothing. I heard him slip in a word or two now and then, when he talked to his brothers about something he didn't want us children to understand, or when he greeted family—*Messiah am!*—as they stepped through our threshold at Easter. And he'd repeat a common saying of my grandmother's, which translates: "A thousand, but not another thousand," meaning, I guess, the earthly years we have left. My aunt at ninety-four says hoarsely, "We weren't like the children in the city—we didn't hear Arabic every day. All our neighbors spoke English, so we spoke it, too."

If my father knew next to nothing of Arabic, I know even less. Really, just the names of food—kousa, shish kebab, baclava, hummous, tabbouleh—pronounced flatly without the gutturals anyone comfortable in the language would lend them. As a child I was taught to make traditional Lebanese dishes; to hollow out kousa—a pale green, sweet summer squash we stuff with lamb and rice and steam over a bed of scrap bones; to cover phyllo dough with a damp towel—the unbaked pastry was thin as gauze and ruined by the open air—as I built up buttery layers of baclava. To drizzle the hummous with oil, and sprinkle it with paprika, and ring it with slices of red onion before serving. I learned from my mother, who knew nothing of Lebanese cooking until she married and moved out to the farm where she was taught by her mother-in-law to make the things my father loved.

By the time I was school-aged, my mother was an expert at it. She and I would sit at the kitchen table and hollow out one kousa after another. The squash was soft and slender, and the shell had to be thin and even in order to cook well. I was a child, impatient and awkward with the corer. My mother went over my work after she'd finished hers, paring more squash off the thick places and patching my holes with bits of the inner flesh, before she filled all the kousa with lamb and rice.

Chopping, paring, coring, rolling, simmering. Slow, attentive work—without connotation or inflection—more easily passed along than language, with less to misunderstand. And once learned, something that comes back after years, long after words have been lost. Still, measured by detail and consistency; and never think such work wasn't judged at every family gathering in the resistance of a fork, in the crumbs that were left behind.

A few years back, before my mother tired of cooking altogether, she began to talk about trying out new recipes. For decades she had more or less cooked the same dozen or fifteen dishes for the family: some Lebanese, some Italian, some drawn out of the New England past of franks and beans and clam chowder, the American present of hamburgers on the grill. She looked to me for advice: "What could I do with the roast?" she'd ask, not in a determined way, but quiet and speculative, as she unpacked her groceries. Or, "You know about herbs. What could I add to the chicken?" I felt the same sting as when I first notice a burnish on the September leaves. "You know plenty of ways to cook chicken," I'd said awkwardly, feeling I'd traveled too far. I walk so much faster than her now, and arrive everywhere first.

I have to slow my pace consciously as we walk up the steps of the Melkite church for my father's forty-day Mass. We're here more for the gesture to the old Lebanese community than any church vigilance on my father's part. He'd have trouble sitting still for this, especially since, for the convenience of the relatives who have to travel a ways, we've settled on the late Mass, which is sung in Arabic. As I enter the church, I can smell the incense from the earlier services. My eyes are drawn upwards to the iconostasis that divides the altar from the people: a row of paintings of the angels and saints—straight-nosed, almond-eyed, heads tilted under gilt nimbuses—Byzantine, accomplished without perspective. Flat and shimmering, made of wood and mineral, egg, alabaster, and pigments ground fine as the dust of relic bones, they're meant to illumine another world, and separate us from it.

The priest shakes the censer and the incense begins to sting my eyes. The prayer candles flicker. Three men to the right of the altar begin to sing in Arabic. Their voices start low and move up to an extended nasal waver, blending and carrying the music forward, voices singing as they have over the long line of the dead, ours and others, no matter the soil. Once the priest begins the Mass, the three men lead the congregation in Arabic responses. I can't say a word, but I welcome that language—incomprehensible to me on the page, in the ear—

more beautiful and comfortable than the translation of the stern dogma I'd long ago turned my back on. The priest, I know, is singing of the unrelieved suffering of this world, and how everything exists for the next. I remember how my father loved the things of this earth. I close my eyes and hear only the pure beauty of those resonant voices. Long after they stop, their sound continues ringing in the small church, ringing, then decaying like anything held and left to itself—a whole note, love, or belief.

II

The sun rarely shines in history, what with the dust and confusion.

—Thoreau

8

In the Current

MY FATHER ALWAYS REMEMBERED A HOT, muggy inland summer sometime in the twenties. The river-bank beyond the hills to the south of the farm was dry and dusty. The trees and grass, coated with dust. A boy—white-skinned, arms sinewy from work—grasped a rope swing and let himself fly out over the water. At the highest, farthest point of flight he flung himself away—trees blurred in the rushed descent, the river swallowed him, then brought him back to the surface. When he climbed back up on the bank, he was covered with brown-black oil. "He looked like an-other creature," my father said. During those minutes on shore countless ephemeral things in the current glimpsed by and were gone. The boy reached for the rope again and flung himself in the air, then into the oil and dye and scour-streaked Merrimack.

9

White Mountain Snow Dissolved

IT WAS ALREADY THE WATER OF SQUAM AND Newfound Lake and Winnepisiogee, and White Mountain snow dissolved, on which we were floating, and Smith's and Baker's and Mad rivers, and Nashua and Souhegan and Piscataquoag, and Suncook and Soucook and Contoocook, mingled in incalculable proportions, still fluid, yellowish, restless all, with an ancient ineradicable inclination to the sea, wrote Henry David Thoreau of the Merrimack River, which he and his brother, John, traveled upon in the late summer of 1839.

While reading Thoreau's account of his journey in *A Week on the Concord and Merrimack Rivers,* I've wondered again and again how so much could have come and gone in the hundred and fifty or so years since they sailed home free with a September wind carrying them. The farms that defined the banks of the river, where they stopped to buy bread or melons, where they slept at night, are almost all certainly gone. The barges hauling lime and wood and brick— gone too. And whole worlds that had barely emerged when they sailed have flourished and passed. The textile industry that Thoreau witnessed in the incipient city of Lowell in 1839 eventually spread to cities on nearly every drop along the lower river, cities that brought immigrants here from the Middle East and Europe and Canada whose names and languages still swirl in the valley air. The red brick factories of that industry were so imposing and insistent that we still live with the idea of them though the looms have long since fallen silent, and the cities have become other cities, and the Merrimack itself claims a far more modest place on the map of the country than it had when Francis Cabot Lowell and the Boston Associates scoured its lower length for industrial possibilities. More modest and far, too, from the river that William Wood, chronicler of the New World, described for future voyagers in the early seventeenth century: *All along the river side is fresh marshes, in some places three miles broad. In this river is sturgeon, salmon, and bass, and diverse other kinds of fish. To conclude, the country scarce affordeth that which this place cannot yield....*

As the Merrimack gathers its waters and its snowmelt, it descends through the worn slopes of New Hampshire's White Mountains past granite outcrops and hemlock, cone-heavy white pine, birch, maple, beech, through the cities of Concord, Manchester, Nashua, and into Massachusetts, where it bends eastward at the city of Lowell, and then, for the last thirty lateral miles of its journey to the Gulf of Maine, traverses the low rolling hills of a coastal plain. The bend in the river lies to our west, and this town is set among the hills on the northern bank, just past the inner crook where the Merrimack turns towards the sea.

On the early maps of New England—*being the first that ever was here; cut and done by the best Pattern that could be*

had, which being in some places defective it made the other
less exact: yet doth it sufficiently shew the Scituation of the
Country, and conveniently well the distance of Places—the
Merrimack appears as a central spine rising out of ship-laden
waters, rising then branching off beyond the northern lakes
and into the wine hills. The bend in the river is hardly discernible, and this town doesn't yet exist. You can clearly see
how the first colonial settlements in the lower valley had
spread out south and west of the river, the broad waters of
which had been a barrier to the settlement of the north bank.

The Pawtucket Indians, early inhabitants of this place,
called it *Augumtoocooke*—the wilderness north of the Merrimack—a name it was known by until its seventeenth-
century mapping, when surveyor Jonathan Danforth's plats
divided twenty-two thousand acres into reserved lands and
official grants for a handful of families and their descendants.
The southern boundary was marked entirely by a calm
stretch of the river. The first faint paths of settlement led to
and from the ferry crossings.

Drawcutt, Draycott, Draycote, Dracut. 42° 41′ latitude,
71° 19′ longitude. Straight lines drawn across fishing places
and hunting grounds. Boundaries marked by white oaks and
brooks, by granite blocks and heaps of stones. Their plowing
and planting and clearing, the modest homes they hoped
would be permanent, the plat itself, marked the passing of an
earlier world, though by the time Danforth drew his map the
Pawtucket Indians were already a remnant tribe. Explorers
and fur traders had, years earlier, made their way up the river
bringing European disease with them. Between 1614 and
1617, more than three quarters of the Pawtuckets died of a
sickness, still guessed at, that killed within three days of its

first symptoms: *The living were in no wise able to bury the dead.... hundreds without burial or shelter, were devoured as carrion by beasts and birds of prey, and their bones were bleached by the sun.* They who'd trod paths along ridges and across the valleys, who'd found the shallow places to ford streams and the safest route to the sea, their paths were narrow—*unmapped, unmarked except in the atlas of memory*—and worn so deep by years of use that some are said still to be visible in parts of southern New England.

Brown ink washed out on parchment, black lines on bond. All the maps and all the dissolutions of time that render them inaccurate—scouring rains, disease, invasions, wars and floods. Since the Danforth plats, the wilderness north of the Merrimack has been mapped and mapped again with topographic surveys, road maps, charts of the watershed and the milkshed, soil maps that follow the geological logic of the ice ages and have no center, assessors' maps squaring off the place to account for the ownership of every inch, zoning maps dividing the plots for purpose and use. Each illustrates a small part of the story and none begins to tell the whole.

Thoreau wrote of his own unnavigable Concord River: *it was thought by some that with a little expense in removing rocks and deepening the channel, "there might be a profitable inland navigation." I then lived somewhere to tell of.* Well, if profit and industry mark a place, then red brick cities—count westward and then northerly against the current: Haverhill, Lawrence, Lowell, Nashua, Manchester, Concord—that stand at each drop on the Merrimack make this somewhere to tell of. The same water flows through each city, and by the mid-nineteenth century the same was diverted and harnessed to turn the wheels of the Amoskeag in Manchester, and harnessed again for the mills of Lowell, and, after a brief, nearly noiseless journey along our southern border, again for the mills of Lawrence where my mother's father spent and finished his years as a weaver. The city of Lawrence covers an area smaller than any of the surrounding towns, no larger in circumference than one could walk in a day, yet it once wove the world's worsteds, and still in the air is the litany of mills that came and went over a hundred years of speedups, slow-downs, fires, accidents, and strikes: the Pemberton, the Arlington, the Ayer, the Everett, the Wood, the Pacific . . .

Even if we've come to accommodate them now, the short dense histories of the Merrimack cities hadn't grown out of the local needs of the farming communities and didn't fold easily into the land or the life of the surrounding towns and farms. Though the cities were cut out of town properties, they were conceived as centers for the export of fabrics all over the world, as investments for the fortunes of Lowell, Cabot, Appleton, Abbot, Lawrence—names that mark our maps again and again, having mixed with settlement names: Andover, Methuen, Boxford. And Algonquin: Merrimack, Passaconaway, Wamesit, Wannalancit. One day the mill sites had been mapped as open and green—just as here. Nearly the next, a grid of streets worked out from red brick banks. In 1820 the world at the bend in the river was made up of scattered houses and barns, pastures and stone walls, a sawmill. In the late summer of 1823, the place was called Lowell, and the first cotton mill began operation. By 1837 eight textile firms employed six thousand women and eighteen hundred men who produced nearly a million yards of cloth a week. By 1840 it

was the second largest city in Massachusetts. Twenty thousand souls.

Each of the early cities on the river seemed to sprout up at
least as quickly. When Thoreau sailed near Amoskeag Falls
where the city of Manchester, New Hampshire was being
built, he and his brother made *haste to get past the village
here collected, and out of hearing of the hammer which was
laying the foundation of another Lowell on the banks.* When
he set down the account of his journey years later, he recalled:
*At the time of our voyage Manchester was a village of about
two thousand inhabitants, where we landed for a moment to
get some cool water.... But now, after nine years, as I have
been told and indeed have witnessed, it contains sixteen
thousand inhabitants. From a hill on the road between Goffs-
town and Hooksett, four miles distant, I have since seen a
thunder shower pass over, and the sun break out and shine on
a city there, where I had landed nine years before in fields to
get a draught of water.*

Because we are set between the drops in the river, because
there hadn't been power to exploit along these wide-curved
miles where the river deposits more than it carries away, ours
has been a quieter story, one less marked in time, especially in
the eastern part of town where we live, and which, even now,
has retained some small vestige of its agricultural identity.
What do I know of this place's history before my grandparents came? Little more than I can read from the graves or look
up in the local books. Little more than the facts of who settled
where, the names of those who died in the wars, where the
churches and schools once stood, where old pastures had been

walled in by stones. A world made of daily life more than history, really, the world I know best by artifacts I pull from the earth, by glass bottles mottled with prismatic colors, by the blades and tines of old metal tools whose handles have crumbled into the soil.

I imagine the life here didn't differ significantly in its underpinnings from the life of hundreds of other New England towns. During the seventeenth and eighteenth centuries, colonial settlement followed the smaller rivers and streams into the back country of New England. A fall in a watercourse of only ten or fifteen feet could power an overshot or breast waterwheel for a small mill: sawmills; grist mills for grinding meal, malt, and flour; fulling mills that dressed homespun cloth after it was woven—washed, shrunk, felted, then the nap raised, and sheared. Fuller's teasel grew along the banks—the dried heads were used to raise the nap on cloth—and still grows on some of the old sites. Such mills almost never operated year-round—the bulk of the fulling mill's business, for instance, came in autumn, finishing wool that had been sheared and washed in the spring, and carded, spun, and woven in the summer.

Northeastern Massachusetts is so congested now that, except in a few conscientious towns, the original settlement centers are lost in sprawl. A white steepled church here, a barn connected to a farmhouse there, stand as specimens preserved among new developments and restaurants, stores, and strip malls. They're hardly enough to give a sense of an earlier time, but claim their place the way a wolf tree does in a regrown woods: the wolf tree's long branches reach out and up, its crown having spread out in the full sunlight of an open field in the years before the younger trees sprouted up around it. It stands as a marker of time passing and gone, and a share of its beauty is drawn from the fact of its survival, from the fact of its standing still beside the sway of supple birches and the sweep of pines. They startle you, those wolf trees, when you come upon them in the woods. Alone always, and as arresting as the clear yellow eye of their namesake.

But follow the roads that follow the rivers back into the north hills of New England today and you still see the small towns as they almost were; wooden and stone shells of old grist and fulling mills and the rapids roaring beside them. If you walk out and up above the town until the sound of the water falling onto granite is beyond your hearing, and then look back, you can see the way the circumscribed world of stone and brick and painted wood, off plumb as it is, spreads out from the bright, rushing falls. Smoke from the chimneys gets lost in the first light snows of November. The measured flow of water is half-caught and half-free.

The early lives in such towns and nearby farms were adorned with a plain weave, a linen warp, a woolen weft. Stripes, checks, bedtick, damask, web shirts. Women and girls made clothes, towels, sacks, bags, bedding for the family and also sold and bartered their woven goods at the local stores. They broadcast their flax seeds in spring and sheared the wool from their indifferent breeds of sheep whose fleece, if it didn't come near the quality of that from Spanish Merino, French Rambouillets, and English Southdowns, sufficed. Girls grew into young women, then into mothers themselves, spinning by the fire and weaving in the shed rooms and attics.

They dyed their cloth with vegetable colors: indigo, madder, the bark of red oak, the petals from iris that blossomed in the June meadows and gave a light purple tinge to white wool.

With the coming of the Revolutionary War they wove uniforms for their sons, fathers, brothers, and husbands. As one woman wrote: *Our hands are soldiers' property now; jellies are to be made, lint to be scraped, bandages to be prepared for waiting wounds. Embroidery is laid aside and spinning takes its place. Oh, there is such urgent need for economy.* Dracut claimed about eleven hundred inhabitants at the start of the Revolution, including women and children. Four hundred and thirty-nine soldiers went off to fight—proportionally more soldiers to citizenry than any other town in the colonies—a fact marked down again and again in the local histories. Those who remained sent a pair of shoes, a pair of stockings, and two shirts to each enlisted soldier from the town. After the war, in the new days of Independence, homespun cloth became a fashionable mark of self-reliance, so much so that Harvard and Yale voted to wear homespun suits at commencement. Prizes were given for spinning and weaving. Vows were made to eat no lamb and wear no imports.

Today as you enter the Museum of American Textile History in Lowell, the first thing you see on the second-story corridors on both sides of the entry hall is the largest collection of spinning wheels in the world. Hundreds of wheels have been carried from singular places beside hearths and in ells and are now are set one after another in clear glass cases lit from within. Sturdy, square homemade wheels nudge fine shop-made specimens. Small wheels for spinning flax; walking wheels for wool—a girl might cover three or four miles in the

course of a day's spinning. Some are adorned with chip-
carved table ends or a beaded edge or chamfered legs. More
than a few are elegant, without ornament, crafted in one of the
Shaker villages while the scent of lavender drifted through a
raised window. Wheels collected from foreign countries: one,
carried out of Asia Minor, had spun silk and is decorated with
hammered turquoise; another—a Charka wheel, built in a
case so as to be portable—can fold up to the size of a book. It
follows Ghandi's design and is meant to be used sitting on the
ground. It had been purchased by a collector on the streets of
Bombay.

But most of the wheels haven't traveled all that far, having
found their way here from the Green Mountains, the Ozarks,
or an island off the coast of Maine. A few are painted a deep
butter yellow or bright red or ebony; others retain the warm
luster of pine and maple, or the dreaming grains of oak. On
some the years have flattened the wheel between the spokes
or the wood has been gnawed by rats trying to get at the grease
around the axle. Move your eyes just a bit and they can rest on
a perfectly preserved parlor wheel—it might have once been
a wedding present—adorned with ivory bells and finials.

For each one preserved, countless others sit in neglect
somewhere with worms in the wood or a disciplined, turned
leg in splinters. What is the difference between the lost and
the saved? Between the ones left to attics and kindling and
the one bundled and hauled over in steerage by German immigrants? Or carried back from a Black Forest village by a
soldier returning from the Second World War, or salvaged
from a chicken coop, the manure painstakingly scraped off?
Is it the same as the difference between a word lost and a word
caught as a sentence trails off? How can there be an account-

ing of the voices drowned out? What of voices that were
strong when they lived the story, but in the long, later telling
uttered reedy and hesitant syllables?

They say a humming wheel rises to a sound like the echo
of wind in a storm. Almost every New England girl must
have known it, busy as all the fates spinning out the only
line of destiny she knew: *I have got the most of my wool spun
and two webs wove and at the mill and have been out and
raked hay almost every afternoon whilst they were haying. . . . O Sabrina how my western fever rages. Were it not for
my father and mother I would be in the far West ere this summer closes but I shall not leave them for friends nor foes!
Mary and Elias say Liz dont get married for you must come
out here. I shall take up with thare advise unles I can find
some kind hearted youth that want a wife and mother, one
that is good looking and can hold up his head up. Then when
all that comes to pass I am off in a fit of matrimony like a broken jug handle. . . . Tomorrow I have got to wash churn, bake
and make a chese and go over to Daniels blackbering. So good
night . . .*

The next day, too, she had to wind her spun yarn on a
reel to make skeins for washing and drying. The making of
cloth was one thing before the next—just like syntax—and
through all the hours of dreams, resentments, lost thoughts,
and song, everything would come out even and of an equal
tightness, a handsome selvage, a smooth plain weave. She'd
cross-stitch her initials or sign her maiden name in a small
hand in the corner of a towel. She might pen in four or six or
eight lines of verse. Her warp of linen, her weft of wool contained the same durable root as the web of words.

Though the practice of spinning has been nearly lost,

though many of the wheels persist as artifacts tangled under a kindly light, surely it meant something, surely there's a gathered power in all the solitary hours of work those wheels contain. I've never seen a crowd congregate under the bright corridors of the spinning wheel display, though an occasional scholar wanders through, and groups of schoolchildren line up and then move on past the wheels into the exhibit at large, where one room after another displays the journey from homespun through the modern textile industry. Each room is dark to begin with, and as you arrive at its entrance each lights up and stays lit for as long as you look at it. When you step away it darkens again, and the next one lights up, and so on, as you pass through counting rooms and storehouses and mock-ups of the early factories. You make your way into the factory weaving and spinning rooms of the twentieth century, when the spinners, by the time of the strike at Lawrence in 1912, were working fifty-six hours a week for six or seven or ten dollars in their pay envelopes. Always the roving had to be damp and warm to keep from breaking. Lint swirled through the humid air. Such conditions were a breeding ground for the "white plague," pneumonia, and tuberculosis. In Lawrence, a third of the spinners wouldn't survive ten years of such work, and half of those who died hadn't reached the age of twenty-five.

The cities in the valley, like much of the industrial world, could trace a path back to Manchester, England. England, in order to protect its primacy in manufacturing, forbade skilled British textile workers from emigrating and forbade the export of plans or models of the mill machines. When Francis Cabot Lowell, whose Boston Company founded the first mill city on the Merrimack, toured Manchester he memorized the plans for the high-production textile machinery he saw there. What he took away in his memory has become a large part of the lower valley's story, as did what he sought to leave behind: the degrading working conditions, the lives overwhelmed by exhaustion and poverty, the air permeated with cloth dust and anthracite.

He toured Manchester in 1810, at a time when the place of girls and young women on New England farms was perceptibly changing. Within a generation after the Revolutionary War, Spanish Merino sheep had been introduced to New England, improving the quality of native fleece and making it more marketable to the family-run factories that had begun to appear on the smaller rivers of New England. The larger and more profitable market encouraged farmers to turn to pasturing sheep all up and down their hillsides—farmers burned Mt. Monadnock bald trying to drive out the wolves that preyed on their flocks. This larger market also meant a less essential place on the farm for young women. Factory cloth was finer and far cheaper to produce than homespun. As the price of coarse cloth fell, the home spinning wheels and the looms in the ells and sheds fell silent, then gathered dust and were put away.

Francis Lowell reasoned that by employing New England farm girls in his textile city he would be assured of a cheap, dependable work force and the girls would make more money in his factories than they could earn selling their weaving to a local store or their spinning to an agent. By regulating their living quarters and lives, he believed he could prevent the dire conditions of Manchester from taking hold along the Merrimack. And such regulations would help assure farm families of their daughters' safety. Three-quarters of the first workers in Lowell were young women from New England farms. Their wages were half those of the men.

By the time Pawtucket Falls, where Lowell now stands, was dammed to create a mill pond that would assure the factories of reliable power, the river was already a far cry from the one the first European explorers saw as they rowed against the current up a course that crossed broad fresh marshes, its waters teeming with fish. By the early nineteenth century several worlds had been built up along the river, and had waned. Thoreau noted the passing of cargo trade on the waters: *Since our voyage the railroad on the bank has been extended, and there is now but little boating on the Merrimack,* he wrote. *All kinds of produce and stores were formerly conveyed by water but now nothing is carried up the stream, and almost wood and bricks alone are carried down, and these are also carried on the railroad. The locks are fast wearing out, and will soon be impassable, since the tolls will not pay the expense of repairing them.*

Before the world of cargo, and before the coming of European explorers, the lower Merrimack valley was the world of the Pawtucket, the Wamesit, the Nashaway, the Souhegan. River of sturgeon, the Algonquin word *Merrimack* means— or swift water, or strong place. The inland tribes, who depended for their stores on the reliable run of salmon, bass, and sturgeon pushing up the river at spawning season, gathered every spring at even the smaller falls along its course. But Pawtucket Falls, with its drop of thirty-one feet to the granite rocks below, was the most renowned gathering place of the Algonquin world.

The old town history of Dracut says that Passaconaway was the leader of the area tribes at the time the wilderness north of the Merrimack was divided into land grants and holdings for colonial settlers. If, prior to settlement on his lands, Passaconaway had counseled resistance, within a year of the first grants he could see the future, and it was at Pawtucket Falls he chose to speak for the last time. His last conciliatory speech comes down in common books—this speech alone. The words are variously recorded by various Englishmen: *The English came, they seized our lands; I set me down at Pawtucket. They fought with fire and thunder, my young men were swept down before me when no one was near them. I tried sorcery against them but still they increased and prevailed over me and mine, and I gave place to them, I that can make the dry leaf turn green again. I who have had communion with the Great Spirit dreaming and awake.... The oak will soon break before the whirlwind—it shivers and shakes even now; soon its trunk will be prostrate.... Then think, my children, of what I say; I commune with the Great Spirit. He whispers to me now—Tell your people Peace, Peace is the only hope of your race.... these meadows they shall turn with the plow—these forests shall fall by the axe.... We are few and powerless before them. We must bend before the storm; the wind blows hard; the old oak trembles; its branches are gone; its sap is frozen.... Peace, Peace with the white men, is the command of the Great Spirit—and the wish—the last wish of Passaconaway.*

The area tribes never again gathered at Pawtucket Falls. Today water brims over the flashboards of a dam and sometimes splashes, sometimes cascades onto the rough rocks below. Its color, as it falls, runs to old ivory; in hard winters that falling water forms into a ragged freeze. Except at snowmelt, the river at the foot of the falls is so still and low you'd think it couldn't possibly recover enough strength to flow out of the city. Graffiti on the granite. Some trash. Weeds and grasses have taken hold deep in the riverbed. Sometimes I see a man fishing from the bank. Who doesn't wonder as they pass where the power of the Merrimack has gone, the Souhegan and Suncook and Soucook and White Mountain snows dissolved?

Once I drive beyond the Pawtucket Dam, my perception of the river changes in an instant, as if dissonance had collapsed into one long clear note of reconciliation. Suddenly I'm above the flashboards and running on a road out and away, the river beside me is wide, brimming, dark, holding back gathered strength from the north. Steely, impenetrable under an overcast, and glittering under a clear sky, there are days the river there is graced by compensatory white sails. The difference above and below the dam is far greater than the difference between being half-caught and half-free—it's a difference of scale, accumulation, and history. The dam, when it was built, not only exaggerated a geological break in the riverbed. Here in the valley it separated agriculture from industry.

At first, the sight of so many bands, and wheels, and springs, in constant motion, was very frightful. She felt afraid to touch the loom, and she was almost sure that she could never learn to weave; the harness puzzled, and reed perplexed her; the shuttle flew out and made a new bump upon her head. . . . Here was a new place in the world, and it was lit differently. Whale-oil lamps hung on pegs by each loom. The windows, nailed shut, let in a slanting light to rooms that were

69

sprayed with water to keep the humidity high so the yarns wouldn't break. From a distance, a roomful of looms had the same rhythm as a loud heart, but in the weaving rooms the machine noise was an undifferentiated envelope of sound. The weavers sucked thread through the small hole at the end of their shuttles and inhaled lint, sizing, and dyes. That shuttle design—used into the twentieth century—came to be known as "the kiss-of-death shuttle" because of the efficiency with which it spread TB among the workers.

Most of the girls stayed on at the mills for no more than a few years while they awaited marriage, or looked to increase the money they could bring to a marriage, or tried to escape their households. In *The Lowell Offering*, a literary magazine written by and for the mill girls, Harriet Farley gave a sense of that world in the guise of a letter home: *There are girls here for every reason, and for no reason at all. . . . One who sits at my right hand at table, is in the factory because she hates her mother-in-law. She has a kind father, and an otherwise excellent home, but, as she and her mama agree about as well as cat and mouse, she has come to the factory. The one next her has a wealthy father, but, like many of our country farmers, he is very penurious, and he wishes his daughters to maintain themselves. The next is here because there is no better place for her unless it is a Shaker settlement. The next has a "well-off" mother, but she is a very pious woman, and will not buy her daughter so many pretty gowns and collars and ribbons and other etceteras of "Vanity Fair" as she likes; so she concluded to "help herself." . . . The next is here because her parents are poor, and she wishes to acquire the means to educate herself. The next is here because her beau came, and she didn't like to trust him alone among so many pretty girls. . . .*

Many, who are dissatisfied here, have also acquired a dissatis-faction for their homes, so that they cannot be contented any where, and wish they had never seen Lowell. But tell Hester that I advise her to come. . . .

The dry goods stores in Lowell sold gauzes, lawn, and muslin for frocks and baby clothes; marseilles quilting, Flor-entine cloth, and swansdown for vests. Corduroy, velvets, damask. Fabric shot with silk for fine dresses and shawls and skirts. Fabrics named after places in the Far East: nankeen, harrateen, shalloon. Fabrics befitting the glinting city Charles Dickens described in 1840: *One would swear that every "Bakery," "Grocery," and "Bookbindery" and every other kind of store, took its shutters down for the first time, and started in business yesterday. The golden pestles and mortars fixed as signs upon the sun-blind frames outside the Drug-gists appear to have been just turned out of the United States Mint; and when I saw a baby of some week or ten days old in a woman's arms at a street corner, I found myself unconsciously wondering where it came from: never supposing for an in-stant that it could have been born in such a young town as that.* In the mills they wove plain goods out of coarse cotton for farm families in the West and black slaves in the South. A heavy sheeting—durable, reliable, inexpensive—weighing less than three yards to the pound. What they wove was called negro cloth.

The girls and young women were used to exhausting hours of work at home, and the factory workload, which seems in-comprehensible to us now, was sometimes shouldered matter-of-factly: *You ask if the work is not disagreeable. Not when one is accustomed to it. It tried my patience sadly at first and does now when it does not run well; but in general, I like it very much. It is easy to do and does not require very violent exertion, as much of our farm work does.* Still, at home there'd been breaks in work and a seasonal variety. Now their days were confined to hours and bells, and they no longer worked at their own speed, but were subject to slowdowns and speed-ups beyond their control, subject to the demands of the machine itself, closer to the machine than the human: *The Overseers ... are to see that all those employed in their rooms are in their places in due season. They may grant leave of absence to those employed under them, when there are spare hands in the room to supply their places; otherwise they are not to grant leave of absence, except in cases of absolute necessity.* They had become operatives. In winter they were summoned and released into darkness. The first bells rang at 4:30 A.M., the second at 5:30, the third at 6:20. The dinner bell rang out at noon and rang in at 12:35. The evening bell rang out at 6:30 except on Saturday evening.

Still, in a certain moment, their plainwork had substance for them: *I have sometimes stood at one end of a row of green looms, when the girls were gone from between them, and seen the lathes moving back and forth, the harnesses up and down, the white cloth winding over the rollers, through the long perspective; and I have thought it beautiful.*

Many of the young women had come from large families, but they had never experienced communal living quite like the life of the boardinghouses: *Chairs, chairs—one, two, three, four, and so on to forty. It is really refreshing, sometimes, to go where there is only now and then a chair.* The particulars of their world were gone, particulars they sometimes allowed themselves to remember: *It is now that I begin to dislike these hot brick pavements, and glaring buildings. I want to be at home—to go down to the brook over which the wild grapes have made a natural arbor, and to sit by the cool spring around which the soft brakes cluster so lovingly. I think of the time when, with my little bare feet, I used to follow in aunt Nabby's footsteps through the fields of corn—stepping high and long till we came to the bleaching ground; and I remember—but I must stop, for I know you wish me to write of what I am now doing, as you already know of what I have done. Well; I go to work every day ....*

When they climbed into their boardinghouse beds at night and pulled the blanket over their shoulders they may have heard a few whispers near to the timbre of their own voices softly rising out of the same room. Absent were deeper, older voices muffled in a downstairs room, voices separated from their own by years and experience and time, yet familiar and confiding, there when they woke in the morning, there at night, accompanied by the ringing of a cup set down on the plank of the table, or the sound of a log shifting in the fire and falling into cinders that, in breaking up, sounded like the tinkling of glass.

The gaze of the larger world was turned away from those hearths, from the acid soils and the fields turning up stones every spring, from those places keenly recalled by young women in the factories. The farmers' children, if they weren't heading for the factories, had begun to head west for the deeper, richer soils: *I also wish you could see a prairie. You would feel as you never felt before. You would feel as I once did, when for the first time I stood upon the edge of the prairie upon which I now reside. It was about noon of a beautiful October day, when we emerged from the wood, and for miles*

*around stretched forth one broad expanse of clear, open land.
I stood alone wrapt up in that peculiar sensation that man
only feels when beholding a broad rolling prairie for the first
time.... Fancy upon a level smooth piece of ground free from
sticks, stumps and stones, a team of four, five, or even six yoke
of oxen, hitched to a pair of cart wheels, and to them hitched
a plough with a beam fourteen feet long, and the share, &c.
of which weigh from sixty to one hundred and twenty-five
pounds, of wrought iron and steel, and which cuts a furrow
from sixteen to twenty-four inches wide, and you will figure
the appearance of a "breaking team."*

*The children of New England between 1820 and 1840
were born with knives in their brains,* wrote Ralph Waldo
Emerson. I love the furrowed mystery of his words and have
wondered again and again how much and what he meant by
them, laden as they are with suggestions of introspection, possibility, and violence, of a heretofore unimagined world
opening as young women walked into the crowded world of
the factory and the communal life of the boardinghouses. A
world where they sometimes found a kind of camaraderie as
they took over for each other and covered for each other during absences in work. As they reached for an articulation and
understanding of their own lives beyond days of staring into
the machine, they papered the panes of the factory windows
with reading material, wrote poems and stories of their present and past and dreams, and attended lectures: *Lowell Hall
was always crowded and four-fifths of the audience were factory girls. When the lecturer entered, almost every girl had a
book in her hand and was intent upon it. When he rose, the*

*book was laid aside and paper and pencil taken instead. . . . I
have never seen anywhere so assiduous note-taking.*

The durable cloth they wove into countless white bolts
was carried away on wagons or shipped by rail to the new
reaches of the country, was unrolled across a table where patterns were pinned and chalked onto the plain weave, and the
cloth cut and sewn into workshirts. The last hint of salt from
the young women's hands mixed with red southern soils and
deep brown prairie loam as whole families stooped to plant
freshly broken fields. However durable, soon enough the
cloth was worn and bleached and frayed by time and effort
until it was patched and threadbare, and at last cut up for
quilts or rags or a child's toy, after which it all but disappeared.

Yet fragments of those young women's free hours survive in
the letters, poems, and stories they wrote, which come down
to us in brown script or in lead type, in accounts of childhoods
and work days, and in dreams of a new social order, like that
of Betsey Chamberlain's, which she published in an issue of
The Lowell Offering:

*I had closed my book, and sat ruminating upon the many
changes and events which are continually taking place in this
transitory world of ours. My reverie was disturbed by the
opening of the door, and a little boy entered the room, who,
handing me a paper, retired without speaking. I unfolded the
paper . . .*

I. RESOLVED, *That every father of a family who neglects to
give his daughters the same advantages for an education
which he gives his sons, shall be expelled from this society and
be considered a heathen.*

2. RESOLVED, *That no member of this society shall exact more than eight hours of labor, out of every twenty four, of any person in his or her employment.*

3. RESOLVED, *That as the laborer is worthy of his hire, the price for labor shall be sufficient to enable the working-people to pay a proper attention to scientific and literary pursuits.*

4. RESOLVED, *That the wages of females shall be equal to the wages of males, that they may be enabled to maintain proper independence of character and virtuous deportment....*

Betsey Chamberlain lived in the Lowell of 1841, where the working conditions were in decline. Inside the factories, cutbacks in hours during slack times and the slowing of machines meant young women earned less during longer hours. In times of increased production they had three and four machines to tend, and those who fell behind found their wages drastically reduced. They were harassed by overseers who'd begun to receive, as incentives, production premiums. Factory hands were working seventy-five-hour weeks. Wages for piecework had dropped. There were four annual holidays. Such conditions would eventually drive the young women from the factories, forcing owners to rely more and more heavily upon Irish immigrants fleeing the potato famine, the French Canadians hoping to put the hardships of rural Quebec behind them, and the countless others seeking to escape poverty or the past, debt or conscription.

All still to come. In the moment that held Betsey Chamberlain's dream, as the tailrace waste waters rejoined the river, and the factory bells rang across the water, the last Indians living in wigwams in this part of the valley were put on a train north.

10

Five Thousand Days
Like This One

SPEED ANNIHILATING TIME. TIME ANNIHILAT-
ing time. By 1912, Lawrence spindles produced more cloth
per employee than any other textile city in the nation. *At the
time I was just about fourteen years old. We were changing
the empty bobbins, take the full ones off and put the empty
ones in and then start to fill her up again.... And you know
what we had to do? Keep on going and going till night, keep
on doffing all the time, fast and fast. "Come on, the boss is to
come." "Come on, are you still there?" "Come! We got to
keep the thing going."*

In winter, to keep warm, they'd stuff pieces of cloth in the
chinks where the mortar between the bricks in the factory
walls had disintegrated. They'd bring in pieces of cardboard
to place in the broken windowpanes. In winter the streets
weren't plowed, only the sidewalks, since everyone walked
to work. Food was scarce and expensive. What gardens they
had were gone under frost. Coal: some carefully laid it aside
all summer long, storing it in their bathtubs. Others bought it
in small, expensive quantities throughout the winter. Children hunted for scraps along the railroad tracks.

Some of the immigrants had been born in remote places

where, when the snow fell at night, they couldn't see it, though they'd felt its wet flicks on their cheeks and lashes— light, thoughtless—and all night long they'd sense an accumulation in the way the already-small sounds of the world tamped down. *La neva, neige, schnee, snow, snow, snow.* In Lawrence during the strike of 1912 you could see the snow falling through the sweep of the searchlights casting off from the mills along the river. Borne out of the sky, white, startling, furious—by the time it settled on the granite sills and the caps of streetlamps and at their feet, it had begun to mix with soot and ash.

When they left their old countries, the accounts say, their greatest dread was not of any season, but of being denied entrance, of being turned back because of trachoma, viruses, and infections. How do you begin to fear cloth dust falling like snow that never dissolved, swirling in the moist, hot air, whitening their lungs, and burying them from within? *And it was hot. Even in the winter it was real hot. . . . And those old shoes we wore, walking in there, and the floors were oily, and you'd be breathing that lint. Your eyelashes would be all full of cotton. But we knew we had to make a week's pay in order to survive.*

It had been illegal for American industries to solicit workers from Europe, and it was never proven the industrialists advertised, though many insisted that's how William Wood of the American Woolen Company—the Wood mill in Lawrence could process a million pounds of wool in a week—and the owners of the Amoskeag in Manchester attracted workers; others claimed the steamship lines advertised in the hopes of filling their holds: *They had advertised in the newspapers and put out flyers about the wonderful opportunities for weavers, spinners, and dyers in this country. The advertisements they put up were like circus posters.... They showed a man just coming out of the millyard with a wallet in his hand full of money, and he was going up to the bank. A lot of people never even saw a bank in those days.*

Even with meager belongings—papers and change stowed in a breast pocket, a folded envelope of dried spices—when a family reached Lawrence, they'd find there wasn't enough space in the tenements for a world that had once spread across a valley. They strung up their laundry in the kitchen or between alleyways, and their chickens scratched at the basement floor near the coal bins. Goats, too, and pigs kept in the tenements. Young children lit the kerosene lamps, started the stove, and waited for their parents to come home from the mills. And if, while waiting, a child looked out the alley window, instead of an immense and uninterrupted night, she'd see herself reflected in the glass.

Some had intended to make their money and return, others turned on their old life forever, remembering nothing to return to but smoky houses and hard snows. A good many Poles and Armenians and my Lebanese grandparents wanted nothing more than to leave the industrial cities and return to farming even if on unfamiliar soil, and many managed to buy up the dying marginal farms in the valley. Others weren't satisfied anywhere after their crossing. They set sail back to Europe and as soon as the ship left port they began to miss what they knew of the textile cities. When they returned to their old places they might be known as *Americani*, as if the journey could never quite be gone back on, as if in the sheer act of crossing and recrossing they'd lost their place forever and could never be home-staying people again.

Manchester, Lowell, Lawrence, Nashua, and Haverhill each had differing proportions of immigrant groups. A woman from the Amoskeag in Manchester, New Hampshire, remembers: *The spinning room was mostly French, the card rooms were mostly Polish, and the dye house was mostly Scotch. In the worsted dye house, it was mostly Irish. The French people would bring the French into the spinning room, and the Scotchmen would bring their friends into the dye houses. It was the same with the Polish people that worked in the card room. That's the way it worked.... The French people were probably 50 percent; the American people—like the Irish-Americans, Scotch, English—would run probably 20–25 percent; the Greeks would run 10 percent.*

In Lawrence, the mill managers throughout the city saw to it that no one nationality composed more than 15 percent of the work force in any one mill. The older immigrants, mostly English-speaking, held the better-paying jobs. The new immigrants from Southern Europe held the lowest, making six to seven dollars a week, so low that the entire household needed to work if a family was to survive. With enough able-bodied adults to bring in money, there might be enough. Young families had their difficulties, with a mother forced to work and maybe only being able to put in half a week while she left the children with neighbors. Pay and half-pay couldn't feed a family and heat a winter home.

All entered and left the mills together at the sound of the bells. Within, there were countless divisions. The young and the old had their assigned places. Older women, cheap labor, were employed to mount the empty bobbins. Young boys swept floors or cleaned bobbins or delivered materials from room to room. The caustic world of the dyehouses and bleacheries was a man's world—men wrapped in scraps of cloth to keep the acids from penetrating to their skin—where you needed thick hands and strength to wring out the material. Precision and experience in the wool-sorting rooms, which were filled with English immigrants whose hands could feel at a touch differences in length, thickness, curl, and softness of the fleece. A sorting room had its own danger: the raw wool could sometimes transmit anthrax. Young girls were needed for finish work such as burling that demanded precision, good eyesight, and fine, sensitive fingertips. Though it was relatively quiet in the burling and mending rooms and where the woven bolts of cloth were inspected, the work took a toll on the eyes: *Everybody got only so much black cloth because it was hard to mend. That day my eyes were getting watery, and the cloth inspector gave me my third black roll. She was English and I guess she didn't like the Germans, I don't know...*

The accounts of the warp rooms and weave rooms tumble one on top of another: *There were so many black frames and so many maroon; and on the other side of the room where the black dust wouldn't fly, they had the white. Those who worked on the black got a cent more in their pay, when we got out of there we'd look like real Negroes we were so black.... My work was handlooms—four shuttle, four color. Some weavers weave all their lives and never get the hang of it.... I preferred to weave because it paid better.... We tied each end with a knot to a black-topped pin, then we take*

*these pins and tie it on the beam. Each one, even, even, even.
So that everything was close. We had to look all the time.
Sometimes the thread breaks, and we had to piece it up. We'd
stop the beam and make a weaver's knot, just to make it even.
We start the machine again until the beam was full....When
the beam was full, there would be eight hundred to a thousand yards on it.... You had to watch for when the ends break.
You had to know where and why and if the spool was
empty.... If your hands sweat, we had a little bag of white
chalk, because it would stain the silk.... You had to be on
your toes all the time. Watch your clock; watch your silk. You
got hell if you wasted time.... They never wanted to see a
loom stop, because once you stop a loom you're gonna make a
bad mark, you know.... And it was gloomy. I think they had
twenty-five watt.*

The noise in the weave rooms was loud enough to break
the sleep of earth. The whole place vibrated and the workers
would be shaking, their ears ringing as they left at the end of
the day. The money was small. The same thing over and over
as they labored under the threat of stretchouts and speedups,
of grudges that could slow the work down and affect pay—if
the loom fixer had something against you, he'd skip over you
and go on. The mill bells, the mill gates closing at 6:00 A.M.
sharp. Piece rate. There was a premium system under which,
once the required amount was earned, workers received addi-
tional wages only if the work was performed in an unbroken
four-week period. A day's absence canceled their premium.

Even well-intentioned laws passed by the state could make
a winter colder. In January 1912 a Massachusetts law decreased the work week from fifty-six to fifty-four hours for

women and for children under eighteen. The law made no provisions for compensatory pay for the loss of hours, unlike the previous act of the legislature, which in January 1910 had decreased weekly hours from fifty-eight to fifty-six but had also increased day and piece rates to make up for the hours lost.

On New Year's Day 1912, the American Woolen Company announced that workers should expect reduced pay in their envelopes. On Thursday, January 11, the weavers at the Everett mill—mostly Polish women—opened their pay envelopes and saw the money was short. They stopped their looms and stood by their machines for awhile. When questioned, they simply said: "Not enough pay." When the new legislation was explained to them, they said: "Not enough pay." When they were asked to leave quietly, they threw down their aprons and marched out of the mill calling "All Out. Short Pay!" As other workers joined the protest, some slashed belts and broke harnesses as they walked away from their stations. The violence increased as the strike progressed from mill to mill. By nine the next morning the riot bells sounded from the tower of City Hall. Two hours less meant the workers had lost between sixteen and twenty-five cents out of their weekly paychecks. A loaf of bread for each hour lost.

Brot, bread, *pain*, *pane*. *Khoubz* in Arabic. Blessed, thanked for, kissed—like a child's hurt—if dropped. Sliced against one's woolen vest, sliced against the galvanized table top, or torn to sop up the last of a thin sauce. Once stale it was softened again in a salad of tomatoes and onions and oil, or broken into milky coffee for breakfast. Eaten with every meal, or sometimes the meal was bread alone. In the central district of Lawrence there may have been as many variations of making bread as there were languages: a slack dough with olive oil added to it; caraway, butter, raisins; the loaves shaped into rounds or like slippers; braided, flat; the tops scored or sprinkled with seeds; glazed with milk to soften the crust, with egg white to give it a shine. But such variations are always smaller than the whole: flour, yeast, water, salt. When the corner bakeries were going full force, the air smelled simply of bread—yeasty, faintly sour—in the German neighborhood, the Irish, the Italian, the French-Canadian, the Syrian. Not much escaped and roamed freely other than the aroma of bread drifting into the households, here and gone and here again. *Brot*, bread, *pain, pane, khoubz*. The word alone in their native tongue. And theirs alone. Who among them believed *pane* and *khoubz* really meant the same thing?

By mid-January, the governor of Massachusetts had called in militias from Lowell and Haverhill to help keep order in the city. The Boston militia prepared to go to Lawrence as well. What had begun as a disorganized effort among people with uncommon tongues, no more articulate than the two short sentences, *All out. Short Pay!* had become a strike involving twenty-five thousand operatives, forty different nationalities, the skilled and the unskilled, demanding not only an increase in wages but changes in working conditions as well.

Swept along with the deliberate will of the strikers, and taken for supporters, were some who stayed on the sidelines, too quiet to get involved, and some who couldn't go to work because there was no work, or because they were afraid. *You didn't dare be in the mills at all. . . . They'd even come around to your house, and if there was a light early in the morning at six or seven o'clock, they came along and they rapped at your door, and they'd tell you put out the light, you can't go to work.*

With so many languages, at times it was hard to tell a deliberate act from a misunderstanding, as when a Syrian man who was buying milk for his child in the morning was told to go back in the house by a member of the militia. Who can tell whether he disobeyed deliberately or simply didn't understand? As he continued on his way the militiaman struck him across the face and broke his cheekbone. The incident has always stood for resistance, as if once the strike began there could be no small action.

Likewise, there could be no small death. When John Rami, a sixteen-year-old boy, was stabbed in the back with a bayonet during a strike demonstration, his anonymous life became a historical moment; his funeral, a cortege of thirty cars and wagons. A few months after his death he is remembered as "a young Syrian" in records of the Congressional hearings on the strike. During those hearings, conducted early in 1912, one worker after another gave testimony of the conditions in the Lawrence mills. Those interviewed ranged from the most experienced to the youngest of bobbin boys and pieceworkers—boys and girls fourteen, fifteen, sixteen years old who'd never before been asked what they thought, who'd brought their pay envelopes home and kept twenty cents for themselves after giving the rest to their parents for household expenses. The questioners sometimes had difficulty hearing the questioned: *Say that again . . . You have said that so fast*

I could not understand ... In the Immigrant City Archives, Lawrence's Historical Society, the bound volume of those hearings is losing its spine. The pages are brittle. The voices fall through the years:

You asked me whether I supported my family out of ten dollars a week. Of course we do not use butter at the present time. We use a kind of molasses; we are trying to fool our stomachs with it....
    It is a bad thing to fool your stomach ...

Yes sir; there are always some people who are healthier. Those who have come recently from the old country are healthier.... They have red cheeks, and so on. They are apt to find it pretty hard for the first few weeks, because they are not used to such machinery. They call them "devils" and not machinery. After working for a while they are getting used to it, but they say that in England and France they did not do as much in a week as they do in three days in this country.... When the Italians get their pay and see that they never have enough bread, and still their wages are cut down, their wages getting smaller, and two loaves of bread in that pay envelope ... the Italians, going down, you know, they made a little noise; they sang songs and they said, "We are going to fight them for more bread." ... Probably if they would throw a piece of ice or snow, it was because they were desperate.... They were good people; and as soon as they ask for a piece more of bread they told them they are foreigners and that they are all kinds of things.

But would you like to have the law changed so that boys could not go into the mill until they were sixteen?

I would; but what would we eat if I go to school?

How long have you been working at that mill?

About two years. I have been working a few months in the Washington mill and in the Everett mill, and two years in the Wood mill.

Are you sixteen years old?

Sixteen in a few months, or sixteen last July.

Talk louder.

Sixteen last July.

Yes, sir; had to work barefooted there, with only overalls and a small shirt on.

Why did you have to do that?

You would fall; and you would have sore feet if you worked with shoes on . . .

Were you hurt in the mill?

Yes, sir, part of my right thumb was cut off.

Part of your thumb is gone now?

Yes, sir.

You have been working without shoes in the winter?

Without shoes; it is wet there the same as in the cellar.

Why didn't you wear shoes?

Because we can't stand it; it is too hot.

You could have had shoes on if you wanted to, could you?

Well, then we would not be able to work . . .

You say you would not be able to work with shoes on?

With shoes on.

What I want to know is if you had shoes?

If I wanted to put my shoes on, all I had to do was to put my shoes on . . .

*

What furniture have you in the house?
Oh a couple of beds; that is all.
Have you carpets on the floor?
I guess not. I guess some horses lives better than we do.
Well I would rather you answer my questions nicely, John,
and not try to be funny; it doesn't pay. We just want to get at
the exact conditions with all of you people that live in that
city and work in those mills.
Right along that line, Mr. Wilson, I want to ask one
question.
Yes.
I have heard quite a number of you people talk about living
on bread and water. Has there ever been a time when you
were compelled to live on bread and water?
Yes, sir.
How long were you compelled to live on it?
Well sometimes we did not have enough money to buy
bread one day or two days.
That is not very often, is it?
No.

The organizers of the strike knew they couldn't rely on
language alone for success. After they secured representatives
and translators for every group—for the Italians, the French,
the Polish, the Syrians—they gathered the workers on Lawrence Common so that all could see the strength of their numbers. From the side streets and tenements the strikers con-
verged on the spare winter green in twos and threes, alone.
Many who remember the meetings remember the songs—
everybody singing in a different language, songs that ran
around like ragtime, old tunes granted new words: *In the*

good old picket line, in the good old picket line ... The strikers will wear diamonds in the good old picket line. If you ask a group of those who were there what they sang, many will recall "The Internationale." They start off hesitant and slow—*I forget it now to tell you the truth ... If I heard it I could sing it.* But the words come soon enough to one—in French, and another translates behind him: *It's the final fight ... Let's get together—it's tomorrow ... The international world will be the human world ... Let's get together—it's tomorrow.*

The Lawrence Common is strictly a common, without gardens or ornaments. A modest, circumscribed respite lying at the heart of the central district. Once it was graced by elms. Now its scattering of maples isn't dense enough to keep you from noticing what surrounds it—all the squat brick and stone buildings, and the churches: the stone-and-red-door patrician Episcopal church with its stained glass windows designed by Tiffany and LaFarge; the Hope Congregational built with granite blocks left over from the construction of the Lawrence Dam; St. George's Orthodox with its plain, blonde exterior brick sheltering an interior of gilded and iridescent icons. And beyond the Common are what seem like countless churches, more churches than mills—Sts. Peter and Paul, a modest wooden building first constructed as a mission for the Portuguese; the Holy Rosary, with its angels carved out of Carrera marble; St. Mary's, as old as the canals, first for the Irish who built the canals.

Joseph Ettor, arriving from New York, must have known that the city of woolens and worsteds and dyes and scourings and forty-five languages was also a city of alabaster, marble, and stained-glass angels, of prayers to be shielded from suffering, and prayers to be given unfailing strength to bear it. Ettor, along with Arturo Giovannitti, represented the Industrial Workers of the World during the strike, and he is sometimes remembered as an outside agitator, or as one who aggravated the talks between mill owners and workers. The old strikers remember him as having *the eloquence of an Italian and the cunning of a Syrian....You couldn't get away from him when he was speaking.* Whatever else, he articulated the vast gap between what the city's textile workers endured in their daily lives and what anyone would dream their lives to be in the moment he held up a pay envelope and spoke: *This human being, an image of God, gets six dollars and forty-three cents for his week's work. This man has a mother, a wife, and four children to provide for....*

The strike continued through much of the winter. Ice on the river broke up, and the snows melted back from the streets. The workers relied more and more on the soup kitchens—the *laban* and lamb and bulghur of the Syrian cooks, the beans and macaroni and tomato sauce of the Italians. After so many weeks on strike, who could afford the groceries advertised in the papers—the Tunis dates and Camembert cheeses? The children of strikers were sent to other cities to be cared for—an old European labor dispute practice—in order to conserve the dwindling food supplies, to bring the nation's attention to the city, to keep the young out of the fray: *I sent my child away because I did not want my child to see what is going on in the city.*

The Congressional hearings continued. A picture of workers staring down the militia appeared on the cover of *Harper's Weekly*. They say, in the end, it was the wider scrutiny that finally resolved the strike. On March 12, the American

Woolen Company agreed to the strikers' demands. The workers had gained an increase in wages of one to two cents an hour in their weekly paycheck, which could be counted as four loaves of bread, and a little more.

It hadn't the strict measure of an organized parade, their victory march, which appears now, in photographs, as a fluid human line in caps and winter coats. Everyone is walking easily, some are talking among themselves, others must be singing. It's a moment of reprieve in a world of workers who carried with them nearly a hundred years of clothmaking. So much had changed since young women began weaving cheap cottons for farmers in the West and slaves in the South as their brothers and fathers worked the first and second mow in the hayfields and the forests grew back over abandoned pastures and Betsey Chamberlain dreamed that the price of labor should be sufficient, the laborer being worthy of his hire.

Unimaginable, the yards of cloth woven through all the quiet times, and during wars and financial panics and moments of prosperity, as the first cottons—the shirting, sheetings, drillings, and osnaburgs—gave way to cambrics, linens, piques, and lawns, and to blue wool for Civil War uniforms, which were succeeded in turn by corduroys, moleskins, velveteens, silks, and chintz. By the end of the nineteenth century, the sample books displayed hundreds of choices in florals, plaids, stripes, and saturated colors for merchants and clothing manufacturers to ponder. Yet there was little time left after the strike of 1912—maybe time for storm serge, time to supply soldiers with khaki and olive drab and blankets for the cold of Europe—before synthetics came in, and the factories went south for cheaper labor rather than refurbish the old machines for a new cloth.

Much in the making of cloth is a dream of precision. Even, even, even. In the remembering, it's less so. More than the building of the Lawrence dam, more than the daily lives, and wars and epidemics, the ten weeks of the strike of 1912 is the most written about moment in Lawrence's history. A hundred historians have tugged at the same set of facts and statistics to gain their perspectives, to tell labor's version, the feminists' version, management's version, a version roused by speech, a version roused by singing. The Strike for Bread and Roses is what many call it now.

Work created the Merrimack cities, and work was the reason so many came. Still, sometimes the avenues were lit for evenings out. Caruso sang, Charlie Chaplin performed live on stage, Lillian Russell. In winters when the sluggish waters above the Lawrence dam froze solid, there were carnivals on the ice, with ski jumps and toboggan runs and large circles cleared for skating.

When my mother remembers her father she says: "He was a weaver in the Wood mill, he'd tend bar at the Sons of Italy on weekends, and bicycle to his garden plot in Pleasant Valley." I've asked and heard more—she knows more—I imagine he talked more—about his garden than I have of his work in the mills. "He would have loved to have been a farmer," my mother says. By the time my grandparents arrived in Lawrence, the mills covered more than three hundred acres of the city, and the tenements were set as thick as they'd ever be. The demand for housing was so great that the landlords had filled in previously open spaces where small gardens, arbors, and trees might once have been with more tenement housing. What gardens the mill workers had were pushed beyond the city limits to the banks of the river in a place called Pleasant

Valley. With its alluvial soils rich and clear of stones, there are farms on the land to this day.

Among the fruits and vegetables my grandfather planted in his plot were some of what he knew from the village he was born to halfway between Naples and Rome, where the growing season was warm and long under a Mediterranean sun. Everything—peppers, eggplant, tomatoes, basil—was frail to the frost and needed to be set in warm earth. He had to start the seedlings indoors or under glass. He had to protect them in the cold September nights. He had to bury his fig tree every fall, and unearth it every spring and set it upright once again.

They weighed hardly more than cloth dust, those seeds, but they were of a different substance entirely than the world he inhabited all week: the narrow way where the web of carded fibers turned to soft strands of sliver, which were drawn and twisted, and shuttled through the shed of a warp, and beat into their final place. Something to grow and taste and smell of the life he desired.

My grandfather died when I was four and I only remember an old and ill glimpse of him. But I can imagine a Sunday supper—*Sunday was our day* the mill workers liked to say—in the lingering twilight at the end of summer. The late sun, a sheen on all the galvanized things, the smell of the season's grapes, the last of the wine in a cup, his own tomatoes and peppers and eggplant simmering in olive oil. Minced green onions, some basil and parsley. After so many years he still spoke with the rough accent of Caserta Province, the place he'd left before a quarter of his life had passed. After so many, he raised a toast in his old tongue: *Cinque mille questo giorno.* The same every time, a four-word shorthand for *May there be ... may you have ... may we all have five thousand days like this one.*

93

11
Influenza 1918

IN ORDINARY TIMES, THE BANKERS, LAWYERS, and mill owners who lived on Tower Hill opened their doors to a quiet broken only by the jostle of a laden milk wagon, the first stirrings of a wind in the elms, or the quavering notes of a sparrow. It was the height of country; the air, sweet and clear. Looking east from their porches they could survey miles of red-brick textile mills that banked the canals and the sluggish Merrimack, as well as the broad central plain mazed with tenements. To their west was a patchwork of small dairy holdings giving over to the blue distance. But for the thirty-one mornings of October 1918 those men adjusted gauze masks over their mouths and noses as they set out for work in the cold-tinged dawn, and they kept their eyes to the ground so as not to see what they couldn't help but hear: the clatter of motor-cars and horse-drawn wagons over the paving stones, as day and night without ceasing the ambulances ran up the hill bringing sufferers from the heart of the city, and the hearses carried them away.

It had started as a seemingly common thing—what the line storm season always brings borne on its wind and on our breath, something that would run its course in the comfort of camphor and bed rest. At first there had been no more than six or eight or ten cases a day reported in the city, and such news hardly took up a side column in the papers, which were full of soldiers' obituaries and reports of a weakening Germany. As September wore on, however, the death notices of victims of the flu began to outnumber the casualties of war. Finally it laid low so many the Lawrence Board of Health set aside its usual work of granting permits to keep roosters, charting the milk supply, and inspecting tenements. The flu took up all its talk—how it was to be treated, how contained, how to stay ahead of the dead. The sufferers needed fresh air and isolation, and their care had to be consolidated to make the most of the scarce nurses and orderlies. So the Board took a page from other stricken cities and voted to construct a makeshift tent hospital on the highest, most open land that offered the best air, which was the leeward side of Tower Hill where a farm still spread across the slope.

At home the millworkers breathed in the smells of rubbish and night soil that drifted up from the alleyways. Where they lived was low-lying, so such smells, together with smoke and ash, hung in the air. Their heat was sparse. They were crowded into their rooms. The flu cut right through, spreading ahead of its own rumors, passing on a handshake and on the wind and with the lightest kiss. No spitting. No sharing food. Keep your hands clean. Avoid crowds. Walk everywhere. Sleep with your windows open.

They slept to the sound of rain—rain pouring from their gutterless roofs, turning the alleyways into a thick mud, rain on the wandering hens pecking at stones in the streets, rain on the silenced pigeons puffed and caged in their coops. At times the rain was hard, driven from the north, like mare's hooves on their roofs, drowning the parsley and oregano set in enamel basins on the window ledges. Other times it fell soft and fine out of a pale gray sky, making circles fragile as wrists on the surfaces of the canals before being lost to the brown, frothy water there. And sometimes it was no more than a mist that settled in the low places, obscuring the bottoms of the stair-wells and the barrels and the piles of sawdust, only to shift and reveal the same world as always. Then the rain would gather its strength again, seeming to rake their lives all that much harder. Scrap coal couldn't keep away its chill.

A doctor may as well have gone house to house down Common, Haverhill, and Jackson streets, so numerous were the cases. He'd knock, and often his knock would go unan-swered since it wasn't the family who had sought him out. More likely the sickness had been reported by their landlord or neighbor—afraid that the influenza would spread—so the doctor heard a sudden silence within and a face at the window disappeared into shadow. What kept the families from open-ing the door was the fear that the doctor would tack a card to their home warning of the infection within, and the greater fear that their sick children would be ordered to the tent hos-pital. Once there they wouldn't be seen again until they were dead or cured.

When the doctor finally gained entrance—at times with the help of the police—he could find whole families had been laid low, and the sick were tending those who were sicker. They had sacks of camphor around their necks, or mustard spread on their chests, a cup of chamomile by the cot. Whis-key. Garlic and onions weighed in the air. Some sufferers lay in windowless rooms where the damp had kept in the smoke from a low coal fire, and what light there was wavered from a kerosene lamp. Almost always the disease had gone beyond a cough and aches and a runny nose. There was blood mixed in with their phlegm, and they couldn't move from their beds. In the worst cases their skin was tinted blue.

One doctor could see hundreds of cases a day, and in his haste to complete his records, he sometimes left out the ages of the victims and often the names. They come down now in the *Influenza Journal* distinguished only by their address or their nationality: *four Cases, 384 Common Street (downstairs).* Or, *Mother and Child. Baby Rossano. Father and Son. A Syrian fellow. Polish man.* When the rain finally let up and days of mist lifted to bring on clear dry air, the number of influenza cases still didn't slow. Every woman who gave birth, it seems, died. The elderly, schoolchildren, and infants, yes—but strangest of all was how it took the young and healthy, who had never been sick in their lives. Just yesterday they had worked a full day.

The entrance to the tent hospital on Tower Hill was clotted with ambulances arriving with patients and standing ambulances awaiting their dispatch orders. Many were still horse-drawn and the mares stood uneasy in the confusion. The motorized cars idled, and choked the air with gasoline, the tang of which overlay the warm, familiar smells of hay and animal sweat. Everyone wore gauze masks, and there was no talk but orders. *Don't back up. Bring that one over here.* Nurses checked the patients' pulse and color and listened to their lungs. *We need more masks. Find me a doctor. Help me with this one.* The gate was patrolled by a military guard to assure that only the sufferers and those who tended them went beyond it. Waiting black hacks stood three deep.

Every day at 5:00 A.M. a soldier blew reveille. The quick, bright notes parted the confusion at the entrance, and gleamed above the hospital grounds—a far call from a country those patients no longer came from. The general din at the gate may as well have been the sound of a market day in a port city, and they, drowsing on a ship that had pulled away. They didn't stir. It was no concern of theirs, each in his or her own tent, the tent flap open to the back of a neighboring tent. Tents were arranged in rows, in wards, and in precincts, making a grid of the old hayfield. Its crickets were silent. Its summer birds had flown. Electrical wires hung on makeshift poles, and you could hear them swaying in the storms. The soaked canvas flanks of the tents ballooned in a wind and settled back on their frames. Boardwalks had been laid down between the tents, and footfalls, softened by the drenched wood, came near and receded. The nuns' habits swished. What country was this? A cough. A groan. The stricken tossed in their fevers. Their muscles ached. One moment they had the sweats; the next, chills. In forty-five different languages and dialects they called for water and warmth.

Many were cared for in words they couldn't understand. The student nurses and the Good Shepherd Sisters spoke English and French, but to the Germans and Italians and Syrians their voices may just as well have been more soft rain. A face half-covered with gauze leaned near their own. They were given water to drink. Cool cloths were placed on their brows. They were wrapped in blankets and wheeled outside for more air. Someone listened to their hearts, and then to their bogged-down lungs. A spoonful of thick serum was lifted to their lips. Their toes and fingertips turned blue from lack of oxygen. In many pneumonia set in.

It was the same suffering in each tent, in each ward, in each precinct of the hospital. And the same in the surrounding country, in all cities, in all the known nations of the world. It struck those already stricken with war, in the military camps, the troop ships, the trenches, in the besieged villages along the Meuse, in the devastated plain called the Somme, in the Argonne woods. It struck those who knew nothing of the war— all the Eskimos in a remote outpost, villagers in China. Some died without having given it a name. Others called it "the grippe," the flu—influenza—meaning "under the influence of the stars," under Orion and the Southern Cross, under the Bear, the Pole Star, and the Pleiades.

When care failed in the Tower Hill hospital the Good Shepherd Sisters closed the eyes of the dead, blessed the body in the language that they knew, blessed themselves, and closed the tent flap. The sisters on the next shift said a last prayer in front of each closed tent and turned to the living.

In the central city, those who were spared became captive to a strange, altered music. All the sounds of their streets— voices and songs, teams hauling loads over paving stones, elm whips cracking the air and animals, bottles nudging one another in the back of a truck, the deliberate tread of the iceman on their stairs—all these were no longer heard. Or weren't heard as usual. Survivors strained at the absence as if they were listening for flowing water after a cold snap, water now trapped and nearly silenced by clear ice. Schools and movie houses had been ordered closed and bolted shut; public gatherings were curtailed. Workers, their numbers halved, walked down Essex Street to the mills in a slackened ribbon. Their tamped-down gossip touched on only those who had been stricken, who had died in the night. They traded preventions and cures, some wearing masks, others with garlic hung around their necks. More pronounced than the usual smells of the fouled canals or lanolin or grease were the head-clearing scents of camphor and carbolic soap.

The flow of supply wagons slowed as well. There was no commerce in bolts of velvet, silk puffs, worsted suits, or pianos. Bakers who used to shape one hundred granary loaves a day—split and seeded and washed with a glaze of milk—took to preparing fifty or sixty unadorned loaves. In the corner groceries, scab on the early apple crop spread, grapes softened then soured, and pears turned overripe in their crates.

The absence filled with uncommon sounds. Children with nowhere to go played in the streets and in the parks as if it were another kind of summer. They sang their jump rope songs and called out sides in the letups between rain. The pharmacies swarmed with customers looking for Vaporub, germicide, and ice. And all the carpenters—whether they had formerly spent their days roughing out tenements or carving details into table legs—had turned to making pine boxes. Their sawing, and the sound of bright nails driving into soft wood, could be heard long into the night. Even so, coffins remained scarce and expensive.

The streets running up to Tower Hill rushed with ambulances, police cars, and fire engines. The alleyways and side streets were clogged with passing funerals. Meager corteges were everywhere—there, out of the corner of an eye, or coming straight on. In hopes of slowing the spread of the epi-

demic, the Board of Health had limited the size of the funerals to one carriage. They prohibited church services for the
dead, and forbade anyone other than the immediate family to
accompany the coffin. So, a black hack or a utility wagon with
a loose knot of mourners following on foot behind was all.
Some of the grieving were sick themselves, some barely recov-
ered, and they had trouble keeping up if the hack driver was
proceeding faster than he should—there were so many, had
been so many, and someone else was waiting for his services.
The processions appeared to be blown by a directionless
wind down home streets past the millworks and across the
bridge to the burial grounds on the outskirts of the city.

The mourners entered a place starred with freshly closed
graves and open graves with piles of earth next to them—clay,
sea-worn gravel, sodden sandy loam. The gravediggers kept
on shoveling—they had long stopped looking up from their
work. Even so, they couldn't stay ahead, and most of the
coffins were escorted to the yard and left near the entrance
along with others to await a later burial. Few of the processions were accompanied by ministers or priests. The parents
or children or sisters of the deceased bowed their heads and
said their own prayers. Perhaps they threw a handful of earth
on the set-aside box. Maybe they lay a clutch of asters on the
top. So plain and unsacred, it may just as well have been a
death in the wilderness. Small. A winter spider crawling
across an old white wall.

"We knew it was serious, but we didn't know how serious," my father said. The farm is less than five miles to the
west of Lawrence, but by the time news reached here, it was
muted and slowed—no more than a rumor on the sea winds

biting in from Cape Ann. Their eastward view was open then, and they could see the leeward slope of Tower Hill, though it was far enough away to appear plainly blue. On the first of October 1918 they woke to see the flanks of those white canvas tents set in columns and rows across the hill. And that night the horizon was so crowded with lights that it must have seemed as if the heart of the city had grown closer.

As in the city, whole families on some farms were stricken, others spared. His family was spared—all he knew of the flu then was white chips of camphor in an old sock around his neck, and his mother whispering to his father in the evenings: "You'll bring it here." His aunt and uncle, who had a nearby farm, and his cousins all came down with it in their turn, until the whole household was confined to their beds. No doctor came. My grandfather, after he had tended his own herd, saw to theirs—to their water and feed, and to their milking. He drew water for the house and brought them bread. He'd light the fires and bring in a day's supply of wood. Even so, with the windows open, the rooms felt cold as quarried granite.

The youngest boy died. The parents, still weak, were slow to perform the offices of the strong. They washed the body and had to rest. It seemed to take most of a day to make a respectable, small pine coffin. They cleaned the front room, set the coffin in the bay window, and took their turns sitting beside it. Not even small things were the same. Not the rust-colored chrysanthemums blooming against the kitchen door. Not the lingering fragrance of thyme and mint in the yard.

And the large things to be done—the work that had waited all through their sickness—waited still and weighed heavier. It was late enough in the year so that the weeding didn't matter anymore. But carrots, potatoes, cabbages had to be harvested and stored. Wood to be gotten in. The late apple tree was laden with fruit—the Ben Davis apples would cling to the branches all winter if you let them. Enough work to fill their days for as long as they could foresee.

There are two small, walled-in graveyards in the middle of our farm, and they seem odd and adrift now among our fields and woods, though in the early part of this century there had been a Methodist church adjoining them. It was pulled down for salvage sometime in the forties, and its granite steps are now my parents' doorstone. My father would sit on one of the pews when he pulled off his workboots. Now he's buried among those graves, just up the hill, behind a white birch. But in those years only the names of the settlers—Richardson, Coburn, Clough—had been chiseled into the stones. It wasn't a place for recent immigrants to be buried, so his uncle's family walked behind the coffin to Lawrence and set their child beside all the recent victims in the city. The mounds of earth beside the open graves were compiled of heavier and stonier soils than any they had cultivated in the arid land they had been born to. Impossible to return to that country now, though they said their words in Arabic before turning west out of the gate.

For another week after the funeral they could still see the tents, white in the new days, just as yesterday. Then at the end of October the epidemic broke, the fires were banked. The tent hospital was taken down in a driving rain, and the stricken were moved to winter quarters at the General Hospital. At night Tower Hill once again appeared darker than the night sky. Predictable quiet returned to the neighborhood of mill owners, bankers, lawyers. The schools opened again, then the theaters. The policemen and firemen took off their gauze masks. On the twelfth of November, the Red Cross workers marched in the Victory Day parade. When the city looked up they counted more dead of the flu than of the war.

The winter of 1918 was so cold the water over the Lawrence dam froze and had to be dynamited. The following spring, the field where the tent hospital had stood was seeded in hay. It was mown that summer, and winds swept the timothy and redtop. Here, after the child had become bone, a liturgy was said for him. A child whose life is no longer given a name or a length, so short it is remembered by the one fact of his death.

On summer evenings, my father would sit on his porch, looking into our own horizon. The long simple line of the hill was gone. Pine and maple had grown up, and buildings squared off against the sky. Once in a while out of nowhere he'd mention the lights of the tent hospital as if he could still see them, strange and clear.

12

The Pure Element of Time

*... one shared it—just as excited bathers share shining
seawater—with creatures that were not oneself but
that were joined to one by time's common flow....*

—Vladimir Nabokov

FOR SOME THE MILL YEARS WERE A CURSE. THE
hurt silenced them, or their spirit. Others will say *that was our
life*, though the longer and larger purpose of all their work was
so their children wouldn't have to live the same. Sometimes
it's those children who remember, and the anger rests in them:
*I'd be walking to Lowell High in the morning. It was right
across the river from where I lived. And the steam from the
mill would be floating over the bridge. And in the winter it
was so cold that the steam would form tiny little snowflakes
that would fall over me. And every time I'd walk across that
bridge and saw those snowflakes falling on me, I'd think of
my mother in those wretched mills.*

The late voices, the last voices most commonly set down,
the ones closest to us, won a certain strength after the ten-hour
movement and the strike of 1912, of 1919 in Lawrence, of 1922
at Amoskeag ... After all the speedups and slowdowns and

recalibrations of the years, they had arrived at a humane place, and then the economy carried it away. A few of the last can be mournful—whatever else, those mills finally put enough bread on their table. And when they remember—speaking not to each other but to a future—they speak into winter-clear air with its shining ring: *You go up and down the aisle, and you say, "I used to have all these looms to fill." Now you don't have anything. Now it's so empty you can almost hear the stillness come across the room. You go through a section where a lot of them are running, and then you come to where it's awful quiet. Only a few are running. And it's a lot colder, too. People don't say very much when they're leaving. They're sad, and a lot of them cry. It's a bad thing when there are no jobs to be had.*

History no longer runs along the river—commerce and industry have turned to the highways—and some of the most densely crowded parts of Lawrence's tenement district—the places where kitchen utensils hung on the outside clapboards and were shared among families—have been lost to urban renewal. My grandfather had insisted on living on the third floor of the tenement because of the better air, and now that third floor where he drank his coffee and dipped his bread in olive oil, where my grandmother made *pizzele* and *zuppa di scarola* while my mother studied the rules of English grammar, is all air.

Along the waterways of Lawrence, the mill buildings, like the old farms of the valley, stand in stages of use and disuse. Some—their windows freshly glazed, the bricks newly pointed—house computer industries, outlets, warehouses, and even a synthetic textile trade. Others are spalling brick and broken lights. New immigrants continue to come—from Asia and the Latin countries now—and are settling in differing proportions in each city along the Merrimack. Most Cambodians have settled in Lowell, while currently over 40 percent of Lawrence's population is Spanish-speaking, mainly from the Dominican Republic and Puerto Rico.

My father once said if our place is still a farm years from now, a Cambodian will own it. But the land values are simply too high for this farm to be bought by anyone as a farm, so when it changes hands it will become something else. Still, however different from the world of nineteenth century immigrants, however much the landscape has changed, sometimes the desires can feel nearly the same. I remember a man coming by the farm looking for work at the start of the year—I strained to understand what I could of his Spanish and his broken English—and I was startled when he said, *I hope to move to Lawrence in April.*

Older residents of Lawrence keep the city they knew in the atlas of memory. The languages and dialects—the forty-five or fifty or sixty—that they'd spoken in the weaving rooms and dyehouses aren't heard anymore. The banks, department stores, and restaurants they knew have gone to suburbs or fallen to chains. They say, *Downtown is gone.* Essex Street, where they shopped for clothes and secured their mortgages and drank their coffee, is half boarded-up. And on the side streets of the city is the main street of another life, bright with its own wares, lit for its own evenings out, and the old weavers and loom fixers can't read the storefront signs on the tenfooters—just above eye level—written in Khmer and Chinese and Spanish. *They don't remember the mills* . . . That particular *they* of the other, you hear it all the time. Even in praise: *You know some of them are really good workers.*

But the old people don't have to look to newcomers for in-comprehension. The history here has moved so swiftly one generation seems to share little enough with the next. Their children may still understand the first languages but don't speak them beyond the household, and sometimes talk as if their parents weren't there: *They live such a restricted life. I told them they should go to Florida for the winter. We've moved beyond our parents, as was wanted. When I talk about my work in the mill,* says a woman who worked in the Amoskeag in Manchester, *to my daughters especially, they think it's a story; and when I say something about living on a farm, to them it's a story. They don't believe it's true that we were that backward.*

The smell of bread still drifts through the streets. Flour, water, yeast, salt. In the Syrian bakeries the fires are as white hot as they've always had to be to form pockets in the flat loaves. The old wood-fired ovens, fed with second-growth New England forests, must have burned far more wood in a year than many outlying farmhouses together. In the intense heat of the fires the loaves puffed up hollow in the center. Once out of the ovens, they collapsed as they cooled, and the baker wrapped the bread in towels or muslin to keep it soft enough to fold around an olive or fresh cheese or a slice of cooked lamb.

By the early 1960s, when my mother made her trips to the Lawrence bakery, the ovens were heated with gas or electricity and the bread was kneaded with a dough hook in an over-sized steel mixer. And now, as the bread moves through the ovens on conveyor belts, the children of immigrants name their bread with adjectives: Irish soda, Syrian, Italian, Jewish rye.

My mother used to buy a dozen plain loaves of Syrian bread, and one loaf each of fancier flatbreads still eaten mostly by Syrians and Lebanese alone, and called by their old names: *simsim* and *zaatar*. *Simsim* means sesame, a bread sweet enough to love right away. Its top is spread with seeds and drenched in a sugar syrup that's been flavored and scented with rose water. Mild and assuaging, it perfumes your mouth with its sweetness, and leaves a sticky mess on your hands and lips. Syrup pools on the plate.

Zaatar is topped with sumac. The dried red berries are crushed fine and mixed with olive oil, thyme, and oregano. Oil stains the waxed white bakery paper it's wrapped in, the spices and dried herb leaves on top are black from the baking. Dark as good earth, the taste of earth. Sumac, thyme, and oregano—used sparingly elsewhere—are used in abundance on *zaatar*. One strong flavor on top of another, acid compounded by bitter, the oil binding them but not subduing them. *Zaatar* smells stronger than the yeast itself, and the air is full of its scent long after it's finished baking. Though there's no one in our family who doesn't love its rough flavor, *zaatar* is a long-acquired taste, and I don't see it traveling much farther than the Arabic language has in this valley: a Mass for the dead, the old folks talking among themselves. What few words we speak anymore, we pronounce softly.

Young Cambodian boys swing out and drop into the flat tawny waters of the canals, one after another, again and again.

Dominican men fish for whatever lives in the Merrimack below the falls. When I see this, I can't help but catch my breath. In my bones it's the river we turned our back on. When I was growing up in the sixties and early seventies, the Merrimack was still an industrial tool to carry wastes to the sea, and far from swimmable. Always there were jokes about tetanus shots and skin dissolving on contact with the water, and fires racing across the river's surface. *I remember I slipped in off the riverbank once. Christ, when I pulled my leg out it was purple. Purple for a week!* Those who could went elsewhere to be near water, heading north, away, against the current, to clearer, smaller, incipient streams or to camps along the lakes near the mountains—quiet, shuttered, muggy days away from daily life—up to where the Merrimack is fed, to Squam and Winnepesaukee and Newfoundland.

Since the Clean Water Act of 1972, industrial wastes no longer pour into the river. Its pollution now comes from storm drain overflows, salts and oils from road runoff, fertilizers and pesticides from farmland, acid rain, acid snowmelt, and metals leaching out of long-spoiled grounds. For most of its length, the Merrimack is classified as a grade B river, which means you could swim in it if you wished. On a clear day, with a glittering surface, it can seem like the past has settled with time or has washed away. Crew teams, low on the water, grace the quiet stretches. Speedboats leave long wakes down its center. There are public landings from which you could slip in a canoe or a kayak. I've been startled by something simply beautiful: a flurry of white sails on the river above the dam one high summer day. To be startled at all is a reminder to me of how much I still see the river as I knew it in childhood, a reminder that in spite of the years of change here, and in spite of my own goings and comings, this valley's legacy has worked into my mind as sharply as the keen of the northeast winds.

The newer immigrants carry their own dangers with them. A Cambodian woman who came to the farm to pick beans and blueberries in the height of the growing season wouldn't go into the field without a dagger sheathed at her waist. Her fear was that soldiers would come out of our mild, cutover woods, and she wouldn't listen when we told her it was safe.

These days, once salmon reach the Great Stone Dam in Lawrence they are guided up a narrow channel, caught in a large hopper, then hoisted eighty feet over the dam. There's a window inside the Lawrence Hydro plant—the present-day controllers of the dam—where a man sits day in and day out during the runs and counts. Mid-May to mid-July, the spawning season, twenty thousand fish work their way up the Merrimack. He counts one hundred salmon, which are captured and taken to a fishery to propagate.

It had been taken for granted, the teeming river William Wood saw in the seventeenth century when he set down his observations about its fresh marshes and its bounty of fish. What beauty and ease we've regained over time must be guarded by the continual testing of waters, the dry weather surveys, the wet weather surveys, the search for a balance or forward movement that eludes with every overflow and every melt of the snowpack. At times I think of a man at the end of his tether doing only as much as he needs to stay alive. The electricity is off, his supply of wood is gone, he is keeping warm by lighting one match after another. We say *the wildlife is coming back* as we stand cold and counting each single thing that passes—the hundred salmon, and the twelve bald eagles feeding on them.

One rainy winter afternoon at the Immigrant City Archives I listened to a taped interview in which Ernie Russell recounted his life on the river during the sixties and seventies. He'd built a camp on eleven-acre Pine Island, which lies in the river between Lawrence and Lowell, not far from the six-lane interstate. I imagine he could hear the steady, surflike sound of traffic as, on the highway beyond, all of the north sped into Boston, and Boston fled north. He floated and rowed over the lumber he needed. He stowed seed for the songbirds and scraps for the crows. At night he worked and read by Coleman light, and in winter he kept warm with a wood stove. He saw a bald eagle grappling with a heron, and the cormorants settling on the broken ice of March. He heard owls calling across the February dusk.

I felt I was listening to a man from far away: *Below the Lawrence falls I don't know well, above the Lowell falls I don't know that well, but in my section there isn't anything I don't know: every rock, the rapids ...* He could name the creeks running into the river. He knew there was no pickerel left. There is a world—sometimes large, sometimes fleeting—his voice seemed to suggest, that exists in addition to the obvious one of our own making. I thought of the Bolognese painter who composed still lifes of the same bottles and vases, before, during, and after the Second World War. Painting them again and again, seeing steadily with a changing eye, fixing a dense, earthy thickness, affirming a line until at the end of his life the forms shed their solid lines and are no longer objects but the ghosts of objects. I imagine he loosed the boundaries of form not to negate the hard facts of the time, but to come down through the years to tell something, too, of the life that continues.

In the sleeping cities, once in a while something is raised from sleep. You can see the Ayer clock, at the heart of the Lawrence mill complexes, from almost all points in the city. The largest mill clock in the world, it once called the city to work. It broke down sometime in the 1950s after the textile trade had entirely declined, and for decades its four faces were stained dark at night; by day they were frozen at one hour. Its bell had disappeared.

The clock was restored in the early 1990s and stands prominent and true over a city where everyone keeps his or her own time, where no one again will tie a small, smooth weaver's knot that will disappear into the nap of the cloth. To raise part of the money for restoration, a committee sold the four clock faces for five thousand dollars each, sold the hour and minute hand, and each hour of each day. The children and grandchildren of the old textile workers bought hours in memory of wool sorters and weavers. The hour the workday started was bought, as was the hour the workday ended. A toll for the lunch hour and a toll for the final hours.

These are low cities, and the Ayer clock stands beautiful and complete above ruined mills as if history were born whole with its new tolling. As if history were entirely the overexpanded dream of a nineteenth-century textile city, it claims a place beyond traprock and soils, grazing sheep and fishing grounds. Its clock faces, too near to be moons, are tied to earth with red clay and lime. *You will only get so far,* they say, *you can only reach halfway.* These are the hours, a tin res-onance, low on the register, more precise than time measured by distance, not subject to weather like blossom time with its petal fall swept on a wind. Unlike time told by a candle burn-ing down, or a glass of sand turned, they are the same hours again and again with no end. Here is time as countless men and women have remembered it, its Roman numbers shining into the night. Here is history standing foursquare above us, stopping us, insisting on facts. And we help it by building such permanent things, meant to last, to tower over us, bear-ing their responsibilities, as if those founding years are what we are tied to forever.

Who can bear the thought of the wind bringing the fallen leaves in? We who have chosen our colors—dove gray, dove white, a cool green—who've chosen what to keep, what to change, we who take such pains to make of our brief moment a place in time, who insist that what sufficed for the old lives—the brittle metals, the darkened varnishes—will not suffice for ours. Who isn't afraid of living in a city built by the dead? Who isn't afraid the place that created us will turn its back on us?

Rarely, a wrecking ball knocks a mill down wall by wall, and afterwards crumbled brick litters the yard, glistening when it rains and paling with dust in the sun. More often the lost mills burn. And when they go, they go fast. The beams are wood; and the wood floors are soaked with industrial oil. Years of oil have dropped off machines and belts. It was a young boy's job to run between the spinning floor and the weaving floor, monkeying around in the gears, oiling one machine after another, since oil could keep the crippled works going just a little longer, just enough to keep the pace up.

When a spark ignites the years, and alarms sound in the winter night, the city firetrucks are joined by those from the surrounding towns, and for the larger fires volunteer departments are called in from the coast, from the broad hills of New Hampshire, from small farming villages with one truck, to join with firefighters from the cities and suburbs near Boston in raising their ladders and pumping water onto the flames. Just behind the yellow police line, the sleepy, silent workers are wrapped in their blankets looking at their jobs disappearing before them. And neighbors—theirs are the old wood triple-deckers—are anxious to have their roofs hosed down.

It takes no time for those fires to become the talk of the city and the surrounding towns. When Malden Mills, which employs fourteen hundred workers with over fifty nationalities among them, burned in the winter of 1994, onlookers gathered on the spine of hills that cuts across the valley at the edge of Lawrence. From there they could see the whole city on the floodplain spread out before them. They talked and watched, their breath forming clouds of mist in the night air. *It was just a matter of time ... The place was a matchbox ...* When something large went down the whole hillside gasped *Ahhhh! Jeee-sus!*

I live five miles away from Malden Mills, and I heard of the fire the same way I heard of the San Francisco earthquake—on the national television news. Only then did I look west to find I could see the blaze even from the farm. I pulled a chair up to a second-story window to watch, and I looked

across our fields and woods to an orange glow far on the eastern horizon. And then sparks, and the glow flared skyward—
I guessed a wall had fallen. I smelled smoke, though what I
was seeing and imagining seemed a world away, what with
the snow-covered fields in front of me, and the dark silhou-
ettes of the white pines. The road was quiet; the night sky,
full of star clusters and planets and nebulae, a night so dark
you could see Betelgeuse for the red giant it is.

At Malden Mills they make Polartec fleece, which—
though an entirely synthetic fiber, sometimes manufactured
out of recycled plastic bottles—is meant to look similar to the
shorn coat of a lamb. It's produced in an array of bright
colors—magentas and teals and French blues—and intricate
patterns based on Aztec and Nepalese and Navajo designs,
just as the hikers and mountain climbers who wear it—and
those who want to look like hikers and mountain climbers—
would wish. The feel of the cloth and the method of production may be entirely modern, but the ones who lost their jobs
in the fire had the old fears of a world without work: *It's been
tough, I saw grown men almost crying this morning . . .*

In its aftermath the fire became large. The story of the
boiler that had exploded with enough force to knock out the
sprinkler system, and the winter winds that reached forty-five
miles per hour that night, and the police evacuating the homes
surrounding the mill, moved well beyond the valley, was told
and retold all over the country, and told again when the owner
of Malden Mills, Aaron Feuerstein, vowed to rebuild and
keep work in the city. Senators and Congressmen came to tour
the smoking ruins. The President briefly nodded Lawrence's
way in an hour as bright and bewildering as the fire itself, for
who had turned towards them until that moment?

116

III

It is like what we imagine knowledge to be:
dark, salt, clear, moving, utterly free,
drawn from the cold hard mouth
of the world . . .

—ELIZABETH BISHOP

13

Baldwins

APPLE VARIETIES, LIKE ANYTHING ELSE, HAVE their years, and Baldwins—along with Greenings, Russets, Winesaps, Sheep Nose, Ben Davis, Astrakhans—drift now on the edge of sleep. The trees survive as solitaries along what was once a fence or at the far end of old orchards that stretch across gravelly New England hillsides. A heart-lifting surprise to see a hill like that in winter: craggy, evenly spaced trees with staunch, gray-barked trunks and bare branches crazing the air, the contained red life in them glinting in a cold sun. Commercial orchards won't look that way again. There's no economical way to harvest trees that are so big, and most of what hasn't been lost to housing has given way to dwarf or semi-dwarf trees that bear more quickly, are easier to pick, and can be densely planted to give a higher yield per acre.

And so many kinds of apples, fallen to market pressures, have been replaced by more uniform, evenly colored varieties. In 1920, the prominent Massachusetts apples were McIntosh, Baldwin, Wealthy, Red Delicious, and Gravenstein. Of those, only Macs and Red Delicious are commonly known anymore, persisting in larger markets among newcomers such as Empire, Mutsu—developed in Japan—

and disease-resistant Liberty. Of course, it is better that some of the old varieties have nearly disappeared. My grandfather had to practically give his Ben Davis away—cottony, tasteless—their virtue, if it is a virtue, being they clung to the branches all winter.

But spicy, juicy Baldwins are another story. By late September the apples have deepened in color to a brownish red with a rusty splay at the stem end. Ripening as the fall itself slopes towards its close, Baldwins—a pie apple, a keeper— taste better after the frost. They're picked in October when the orchard grasses have already turned and morning frost lingers in the shadows. As the winter progresses, the skin of a Baldwin wrinkles in storage, but its flavor and crispness hold, and its wine-dark smell fills closed-in cellars and refrigerators.

Here, the remaining Baldwin tree is framed in my bay window. The late light backs it in all seasons, and I watch its changes as I work, and read, and eat my breakfast and lunch. The man who planted this tree also built my small, white farmhouse—he repaired with scrap, insulated with newspaper, saved string, lived a more frugal life than I could ever imagine. Who knows why, but it's this tree that reminds me of his effort and economy and the rough stone over his grave.

Baldwins bear every other year, and the fall feels different to me in the years the tree is laden. This past September, when I looked up one mild afternoon and noticed how the branches were bowed by the weight of their fruit, I felt my first sting of the coming cold season. It's hard to predict what will fist up your heart—maybe the smell of decay in the garden, or the clearer light, or the leaves whirling in front of the car as you hurry home at night. After that first sting the bright peak weeks follow, then the yellows become brown, the rusts deepen, and the laden branches are what you see every day until the harvest is over and the oaks alone have it. Afterwards, bare branches against a big sky, and the light and forms of the world are too hard to dream into, so you get used to the spare, smaller life, and what once chilled your heart no longer has its old power. What is withheld becomes what is beautiful.

And what of things revived? Of all that is hauled forward so self-consciously? The catalogs that come in my mail are full of old utilitarian things elevated, and as I flip through the pages I'm tugged by the orbit of seamed, thick glass milk bottles, wire egg baskets, and galvanized buckets set apart from their workaday purposes and their strength. Dowdy, plain, taken for granted in their former life, in the warmer rooms of our time such square and solid forms have gained a grace and even seem seductive. And nothing is more seductive than the Baldwins offered for sale in every Williams-Sonoma catalog I've received this fall. Along with Spitzenbergs, Arkansas Blacks, and Winesaps they top off a weathered half-peck basket. Six pounds—about twelve apples—are thirty-two dollars, plus shipping. Available in the catalog only. Each apple, polished to a still life, is more perfect than any Baldwin I've ever seen—larger and redder, no russeting from mites, or sooty mold, or frass at the calyx. Called heirloom or antique apples now, they seem to say, *See how beautiful the old life was?*

And it does take time before I hazard to ask how much of that old life I would want with its aches, its silence and remoteness. The ones who lived it can't afford the price of these goods, nor would they ever pay it. More farmhouses than farms remain. The interiors of the ones my oldest neighbors live in look nearly the way they did eighty years back. A salt box and tea canister by the stove in the kitchen. A plaid wool coat hangs on the coat rack in the hall. The last pansies of the year are set in a milkglass vase on the table. "The younger ones just don't understand," Mrs. Burton says. "They want me to *adjust* since Carl's died. But the world is so different now. I wouldn't know where to begin." Her husband had had a long illness and had left off work months before his death, though they waited until after the services to sell his herd. She pares away the toughened skin on one of her wind-fall Baldwins, going a little deeper where there's a bruise from its drop, and nicking out the rough spots in the flesh with the tip of her knife—apple maggot, curculio, codling moth, all the troubles apples are heir to. It's true, the past is a different country.

In this one a late fall storm gathers its strength over the Atlantic and sweeps in a warm rain. It lashes the bay window and mats the mottled leaves on the ground. No moon, no stars. The bark of the Baldwin tree is silver in the wet night, and its resistant branches toss against each other in the gusts.

14

By Said Last Named Land

As we glided over the broad bosom of the Merrimack,
between Chelmsford and Dracut, at noon, here a
quarter of a mile wide, the rattling of our oars was
echoed over the water to those villages, and their slight
sound to us. Their harbors lay as smooth and fairy-
like as the Lido, or Syracuse, or Rhodes, in our
imagination, while, like some strange roving craft, we
flitted past what seemed the dwellings of noble home-
staying men, seemingly as conspicuous as if on an
eminence, or floating upon a tide which came up to
those villagers' breasts. At a third of a mile over the
water we heard distinctly some children repeating
their catechism in a cottage near the shore, while in
the broad shallows between, a herd of cows stood
lashing their sides, and waging war with the flies.

—THOREAU

THE TOWN OF SLIGHT SOUNDS AND HOME-
staying people Thoreau imagined as he sailed past on the cusp
of the industrial revolution, and all the towns we've been
since the first lands were granted to a handful of families and

their descendants—a spare farming community separated from the world by a quiet stretch of river, a waylaid place between two mill cities, a promise glimpsed in the offing—have slipped into history. Their records and maps, showing lands bought and sold over the nearly four hundred years of settlement, are stained with thumbprints and oils, and the corners are feathered from countless exchanges and handlings. Read closely the earnest markings of those documents and you read a world of boundaries marked by stakes and stones, by the trees and the fences that then stood: *The lot of tillage land on the southerly side of said Black North Road and bounded: Beginning on the south side of the said road at the corner of the wall by the old grave yard; thence southerly by said grave yard and by a wall to the road leading from the Methodist Church to the Whittier Brothers; thence by said road ... thence westerly by said last named land by a fence to the corner in the wall by said Richardson ... to the point of beginning. Said lot contains fifteen acres, more or less.*

To believe we are still a small place apart—to believe in the word *town* in its root sense as a world protected and enclosed—is as perilous as believing the old maps suffice, with their hand-drawn lines describing assessments made with lengths of measured chain, with one eye squinting, tracing stone walls, defining borders by neighbors, knowing in some places the map would be defective and make the whole that much less exact.

The river no longer divides us from the world or brings us the world, which comes in by the road and leaves by the road, and distance everywhere is cut through by time. We are a town surrounded by two interstates. We are a reasonable commute to Boston. What had once been prime farmland, the best going for somewhere around eighty dollars an acre in the early decades of the century, is worth multiples of tens of thousands, and the map we live by now is the zoning map of the town, with its broad, direct lines designating solid areas of residential, business, and industrial lands. The shaded or hatched or dotted overlays, which obscure all delineations of ownership, old usages, soil types, elevations, the milkshed, the watershed, and the grid of roads, describe a world where old terms have slipped their meanings. In early documents sometimes the landlocked woods of the town—old pastures let go to pines, the pines now standing a hundred years—are notated as *vacant land*. Such a term has no place on the zoning map, just as *more or less* hardly fits our requirements for an exactitude greater than paces and strides and weighted observations can measure. Nor can *tillage* exist alongside the current concept of highest and best use, where, for final worth, the assessors reimagine fields and orchards and woods as house lot parcels of one acre, no less.

Such efforts as we've made in these years—on the current map all the land surrounding our farm is zoned for industrial use—will take a long time to go to woods again. Hardly a mile away from the farm is an abandoned Esso plant that had been built—if I read the soil map right—on Gloucester sandy loam: *the weathered surface of a comparatively thin glacial drift. . . . In cleared areas the soil, to a depth of 6 or 8 inches, is brown, mellow sandy loam. . . . one of the important soils, as it represents the best farming land in the region. . . . hay, the most important crop, yields from one-half to one and a half tons to the acre, depending on the season and seeding conditions.*

The rusting tanks of the old plant have been hauled away, but the flat-roofed brick and concrete buildings remain. Moss is creeping up the concrete walls, and mildew stains spread like shadows. A weedy, paved-over lot is scattered with rubbish. It remains a kind of no-man's-land warning the world off with its chain-link fence topped with coiled barbed wire. Signs reading *For Sale* and *No Trespassing* have been up for years, and the place is passed over by developers for old woods every time. I imagine investors are afraid, in spite of assertions that the land is not contaminated, of the future liabilities of building on such land, of what might be uncovered, afraid the work of cleaning the soil may be like cleaning up the river—long and laborious and, even so, not enough. It's easier to break new ground as long as there is new ground. Even the poorest soils keep a time different from human years, the way they build up out of the work of lichens wearing away the glacial rocks, the work of earthworms and sun, of voles and bacteria.

For as long as I can remember there's been a utility corridor along the eastern edge of the farm. I've never known where the high-tension wires link up, only that to our north they disappear into rising hills, and to our south they span the river and continue across the undulating plain towards Boston. This coming year Portland Natural Gas plans to put a six-hundred-and-fifty-mile underground line through the corridor that will bring vast undersea gas reserves from off Sable Island, Nova Scotia, to New England. They'll cut an eighty-foot swath across part of the Maritimes, Maine, and New Hampshire, cut through the southeast corner of our property, and then link up with a national pipeline grid that begins in Texas and works north. Now that six of eight nuclear power plants that once produced electricity for the Northeast have shut down, everyone connected with the project easily says, *You know natural gas is the fuel of the future.* The Canadian reserves will last a hundred years.

Further north in Maine, where the plan veers off the corridor and the proposed gas line crosses farmland and woods, some of the landowners have protested: *How can something be good for Richmond if it's not good for a group of people who have lived there for years? . . . If they ruin the land they'll ruin something we love. . . . I am fighting because I don't want to die in bitterness.*

Because the gas line here goes over a small portion of land already utilized by power lines, it will not encroach on us the way it will encroach on those in Maine. Yet, I keep thinking of those protesters in Maine, though I don't know what to think myself, as the land agent from Portland Gas and I walk the utility corridor at the edge of the farm, finding our way through the brush by following a path made by deer and deepened by dirt bikes. He is a quiet, even man, with all his attention on the job in front of him. Nothing about him specifically to make me uneasy. But with my father's death has also come the unfamiliar responsibility of making decisions and negotiating with the outside encroachments on the land, so even though I don't know what to think, my every word is guarded. Guarded maybe because one of my father's cautions to me was *play your cards close to your vest.* And a little because really I'd just like to refuse every encroachment now that development upon development has been coming in so quickly around us—trucking firms, concrete manufacturing, more trucking. It just seems like too much too fast, and this, too, is part of my wariness.

"We all think, perhaps too much, of the piece of land where we were born and of the blood our ancestors gave us," said Jorge Luis Borges after the Falklands War. "In ancient times the Stoics coined a word which, I think, we are still unworthy of; I am referring to the word *cosmopolitanism*. I believe we should be citizens of the world." I'm always arrested by Borges' words when I read them, and, however much attachment I feel to this place, I also imagine I agree with him. What place, a citizen's duty? What place, the heart's affections? Where does the greater good lie? In a regional decision? In a local want? What choice—to stand with the Mainers or simply let this one pass—I wonder, would a citizen of the world make here and now?

The land agent and I talk about the lumber that they may need to cut, the restoration of the woods, and the price they'll pay for their easement. Orange flags mark the route of the future gas line, and we walk from flag to flag through the marsh across the brook to higher ground. The vegetation that has grown up along the corridor is not like any I see elsewhere here. The electric company keeps the woods back for the sake of the lines, but the land isn't tended or cultivated. Clumps of sun-loving sweetfern—its head-clearing scent rising when you walk on it—run scattershot through the highest dry ground. There's a stand of hazelnuts with their tiny nutmeats encased in elaborate husks. Sweetfern and hazelnuts both will be uprooted when they cut the trench for the gas line. They plan to replant the swath with grass. "They like to plant grass," the land agent tells me. "They know there's a leak when the grass dies."

We come up the crest of the hill just at the old mail road

that runs through the woods. We stop and stand on the two discernible tracks where wagons once traveled across this hill towards the river. In the woods on either side of the corridor trees have encroached on the old road, and branches lean over the last of it, which has narrowed to a footpath. Only underneath these power lines and on the stretch where our tractors still use the road can you make out the two tracks defined over the years by wagons and oxcarts. The road had been on maps hundreds of years back, fifty years back, but on recent maps is no longer marked. "This is where our property ends," I tell the agent.

"I have you down as owning the other side of the road too."

"This is where our land ends," I say, "I'm sure of it." I remember my father in the lamplit circle of his desk showing me this boundary, telling me about the lumber they hauled out of the near woods after the hurricane of '38. In his last year, when I knew he was dying, when I knew many of the responsibilities he carried would fall to me, we hardly ever dared bring up the practical things. Our own deeds are old and inexact and we probably should have had the land resurveyed before he died. But the most we managed was that sometimes he'd unroll one of the maps he kept stored in the ceramic crock in the corner of his office, and he'd show me the boundaries of our property and fall into a story about how he came to own it: *I bought it because we needed wood for the winter. We'd go through fifteen cords. A French Canadian used to come out from Lawrence—carried his own ax—to do some of the logging. I paid him a dollar a day.*

When I think about all that went unsaid while he sat there remembering, I know that part of me didn't want to disturb his stories; it was easier—for us both—to abide their wanderings than to think about the future. If we'd had better maps or had spent more time going over what we had would I be any more prepared for what I've had to face? Always the future is its own bewilderment, and has its own rewards and sorrows. Not long at all since my father died, and already I sometimes feel he wouldn't fit back into this world, that we've arranged our lives beyond him.

"I'm certain this is the property line," I repeat to the agent. "We've never owned that land." He begins flipping through the papers on his clipboard, back past the aerial maps of the property where I can count the trees in the orchard, can see the pattern of waterways through the woods and the clear edge of every field, back past the earlier hand-drawn maps with the stone walls painstakingly set down in a precise hand. He looks exasperated. He'll have to search through the old deeds to find the absent owner of the adjacent land. He begins to flip through more papers. As I wait I look north up the long corridor where the power lines chase the retreat of the glacier and cut across every sea-flowing thing.

After a few minute he says, "I'll have to get back to you." Then we begin our walk back down from flag to flag to the road below.

"You'll put all the stone walls back?"

"They have to restore everything."

A fine November rain is falling, and the dampness makes everything clear as rain falls into the last color of the season, bringing up the red at the branch tips on the birches, and the patchy green of the grass in the warmer places. I see black alder lining the low land along the brook, its silver-black bark shining, its red berries brighter than anything else on the land. Winterberries they're called, because they stay on the branches until spring.

Late every year my father would take his truck down the back field and come back with a dozen cut branches for my mother, a little color at Christmas to arrange in vases and pitchers. He called them foxberries—I don't know for sure why, I've never heard anyone else call them that, but it seems right. Foxberries. By the end of winter they're bird-pecked, and shriveled, nowhere near as brilliantly red as they are in this November rain, but the light is softer and longer then and what color remains is still apparent in the smoky March days.

Surveyor's chains and steel tapes sag over distances. They expand in the heat and sun, so that you have to wait for a cool cloudy day for the best readings, and have to adjust readings done in full day to compensate for the inaccuracies. You need to keep an even stride over a rough road. The fog comes in and you can't see benchmarks or the other members of the surveying team. You go back over the same ground to check and re-measure the work. It is an old trade, and I imagine its earth-bound sounds—the tools clinking and creaking—will grow ever smaller and more distant, quieter, quieter with each successive map made, until they are nearly silent—hardly louder than key clicks.

What will determine our map of the future? The twenty-four satellites orbiting the earth that constitute the Global Positioning System? Each satellite emits precisely timed radio signals. An observer at any point on the earth's surface receiving signals from at least four of the satellites can figure the precise horizontal and vertical coordinates of any point on earth. The waves from the satellites can be read in snow and rain and fog. You can correct errors that have stood for centuries. You can map featureless lands. The only inaccuracy is a slight corruption the government insists upon for civilian use, which will confound attempts to exactly locate sensitive military areas. The map you can compute from satellite readings can be freed from the eye and the subjectivities of the eye, the hand and the limits of the hand. A spatial database has no limits on the density of information. You can add the element of time and can capture the three-dimensional. Some farmers already use the system in conjunction with grid soil samples to determine the precise nutrient needs of every square inch of their fields. They use it to figure potential yield. Precision farming, farming by the inch. *Once you see a yield map you never quite look at that field in the same way again.*

Surely one of those satellites is above us now, tumbling through soundless space, while the land agent and I make our way down the path beneath the power lines. As we approach the road the sound of traffic swallows the hum of the wires. The light rain has stopped. Towards the west clouds have lifted, and the branches and grasses and foxberries are shining in a brief moment of sun. I can't yet see a single star, just that incalculable deep blue of near twilight, vast and peaceful.

15

Storm

THE FIRST REAL SNOW OF THE SEASON CAME ON a warm wind from the coast. Large wet flakes swirled through the brief December afternoon, settling on bare branches, the winter-brown grass, and cold barn roofs. At first the snow dissolved as it hit the black roadways, though by nightfall it started to accumulate there, too, a snow so heavy the wind couldn't shake it loose from even the most supple birches, and its clinging weight began to fill in the narrow crotches of the oaks, it bowed the slender birch trunks and tugged down the upturned, light-loving boughs of the white pines. Only the stout branches of the apple trees refused to yield—they're pruned to bear the weight of a heavy crop—and the snow merely ghosted their limbs.

Inside, the storm built its cocoon of silence until late that evening when the weaker branches began to give way under the weight of the snow. Then I could hear the dry cracking of wood everywhere, and enormous muffled thuds as pine, oak, and maple branches landed on the whitened ground and roofs, on the power lines and iced-over roads, on the polished granite gravestones on the hill.

The power went down about ten that night and in the

greater quiet candlelight brought, I began imagining trees falling in the woods beyond the farm. In their long, slow descent some would snag in the branches of sturdier trees; others, scatter their load of snow on decaying boles—pecker-fretted, crumbling to earth—and on lichen-stained uprooted trunks, rousing burrowed, sleeping life as they toppled onto the last trace of the logging road and fell across stone walls, brooks, old cattle bridges, and frost-withered Indian pipe. All night a falling while my house grew cold, and I slept.

The next morning was clear, bright, and every bit as silent as the night before: we still had no power. I'd never known the electricity to be down for more than seven or eight hours at a time, so I couldn't help but think the power would jolt back on at any moment in spite of such damage: I saw maple branches in splinters. The linden on my mother's lawn had lost three of its limbs—and all its grace—and would have to be cut down. Though not a twig had fallen in the apple orchard, the less sturdy peach trees suffered: some of their east-facing branches had snapped and were hanging by threads of bark. The trunk of the last Elberta had split clear down the middle. The white pines seem to have been hit the worst, especially right at the edge of the timber stand along the old mail road. Where the pines face the woods, half in shadow and crowded by other trees, they're short limbed. But where they face the open road they bear long outstretched branches that curve upwards and feather out to get the most of the sun. Nothing's more handsome than the spreading shape of those branches, but such a shape also makes them vulnerable to heavy snow, since they take on too much weight. Now countless limbs were tossed on the ground, one after another, all down the mail road. And above, where they'd been torn from the trunks, I saw exposed sapwood—warm, honey-colored, out of place against the cold gray tones of the winter bark. I'd see that sapwood all winter long, and it would remind me of this storm, as would the downed pine branches, which remained supple and green, and stirred in the wind as if they still had life in them.

As I made my way across the fields I was as surprised by what survived as I was by what had fallen. There is a solitary standing deadwood rising out of the near woods—a maple, I think—its limbless bole is a sober mark across our summer landscape, its punky bark shreds at your touch, it smells of decay. It had survived intact—a great refusal raised towards the winter sun.

Word was the greatest damage had been here in the valley. To our south they'd had all rain, to our north the snow was drier and lighter, and had caused far less destruction. Here, the radio said, over one hundred thousand people were still without power, and the linemen hadn't seen anything like it in thirty-five years. Even with help from crews coming in from Canada and Pennsylvania, it would take days to get to all the repairs.

Luckily it wasn't cold enough for pipes to freeze, but the thought of being without power for any extended time made other cares stick in my throat. My mom and aunt—what if their houses grew too cold? The old Glenwood cookstove at the farmhouse where my aunt lived had long been given away. It was clear she'd have to spend the day at my mother's house, where we still had a working woodstove, though it hadn't been lit since my father died. Even that last winter he didn't often build himself a fire. That was a sure sign of his failing, since he loved the spot of heat a stove gave, especially after coming in from the cold. As I splintered old shingles and gathered cordwood from a remnant pile on the porch, I tried to remember when it was he'd built his last fire. Sometimes I think of his death and I feel as naive as a child, the way I can't get past the thought that he no longer hears or sees, or feels the bracing January air on his face. *It is strange that a man should be sewn up in a sailcloth and should soon be flying into the sea. Is it possible that such a thing can happen to anyone?*

At ninety-four my aunt has outlived her sister and two of her seven brothers, and I know she fears outliving the others. She had never married, had never—for more than a month or two—lived anywhere other than the farmhouse she had been born in. Now when one of her brothers suggests she spend part of the winter in Florida, she answers, "The days pass here just fine. I sit by the window and before you know it the sun is going down." Though she refuses them simply, she means it entirely. It's nearly all she insists on anymore, having years ago let others take on making her appointments at the Lahey Clinic, filling her prescriptions for her heart medicine, paying her bills, balancing her checkbook. *Well,* folks say, *she took care of them for so long, now it's her turn to be taken care of.*

She shakes her head to think of those years when the house was so full everyone couldn't sit at the table at once to eat, then from the drainboard she lifts a cup and plate and sets them at the far end of the long dining table which she keeps covered in white oilcloth. Morning coffee and toast, jam on the second slice. In the center of the table are silver spoons in a silver creamer. Behind her, the cupboard is full of fine china; the closet, of everyday dishes that have been stacked in place for years. As a child, and then as a woman, she'd spend the afternoons at her own mother's side, slipping proofed loaves of Syrian bread into the Glenwood, or mending workclothes, or shelling peas. She mashed potatoes and turned them into an ironstone bowl, whisked the lumps out of the gravy, sliced the roast, boiled carrots and beans, set out plates and silverware and called her brothers for dinner. I can imagine they'd run straight in after leaving off picking up drops in the orchard, they'd trail in from the barn smelling of hay and dung, from the fields smelling of new earth, having jabbed the spade into the soil to mark their place. They'd drop their homework mid-sentence, or clamber down from the upstairs rooms to crowd the table with its steaming platters that she filled and filled again.

Who would remember anything of childhood without those smells of bread and gravy, without the clicking of knitting needles, or the even strokes of a rolling pin on a wooden counter? And it hardly seems enough now to pray for her easy passage or to say to each other the way we do, "She's doing well for her age," "She's lucky she can still get around," "I can't think of what she'd do if she couldn't live in that house." The house had been standing a hundred years when they were young, and I doubt it felt old then with all the life of the place swirling through. Now it's down to one light, and the clocks all tell a different time, and every change feels monumental. "Why don't we paint the TV room come spring?" I once suggested. "Wait until I'm gone," she answered.

Although the power outage had quickly brought the temperature in the rambling drafty farmhouse down, my aunt— long a creature of her routine—was reluctant to spend the day at my mother's. I had to marshal her out, and as soon as she settled into the chair in front of my mother's stove she promptly asked, "They've no idea when they expect the power back on?"

"The lines to the power company are jammed—I can't get through, I don't know how long it will be," I answered.

She reframed the question half a dozen different ways, and asked it every ten minutes or so all through the afternoon. "When do they expect the power back on?" "You've no word?"

"Don't know, no word," I'd answer again and again, trying not to sound exasperated, as I walked in and out of the house, getting in more wood, checking on things, joining them for a while then leaving to take care of my own house and to do a little work while there was daylight. All that day it never occurred to me to drive anywhere—somehow I thought the wider world was shut down, too. Later I'd read that pockets of the nearby cities had full power and the hardware stores and supermarkets were jammed with people buying candles, batteries, and groceries for next time while we drew closer to the cast iron stovebox and waited for the refrigerator to kick back on and the dark lamps to suddenly stain the walls with radiance. Every moment we believed it could be any minute now. A belief answered with the sound of a candle guttering or a log falling into ash. As we sat, I imagined it was the same for all families up and down the road. All plans set aside, lighting what stoves and candles they had, wondering if they had enough, thinking about the food spoiling in the freezer, whether it be frozen dinners, ice cream, sides of venison, or the corn it took them a whole steamy August afternoon to blanch and scrape off the cob.

In the failing afternoon light we hunted up more candles—the nubs of old tapers and half-spent Christmas pillars. As I warmed up some canned soup on the stove I was reminded how my father would cook chestnuts and popcorn on its top. "Dad would have enjoyed this," I said softly to the air as I stirred the pot, and I saw the pain of remembrance flicker across my mother's face. I don't know if silence or remembrance is best, but I was longing to press a hurt simply to remind myself it was there.

Yes, he would have enjoyed this, and he would have been the one to take care of everything for my mother and aunt during such a power outage. It's been easier for me to make peace with farm and business responsibilities than with this. I've heard again and again over the past year: *Your mother's so lucky to have you*, and no matter who says it—the lawyer, the insurance broker, my mother's oldest sister—they use exactly those words, and their tone is always the same. No other words can make me feel more like everybody's sentimental idea of a good daughter, old girl—patronizing, instructive, always finding a way to surreptitiously check my mother's pillbox, to make sure the doses are measured out and taken.

Sometimes I wish she wouldn't tolerate my care. I wish she could break out of the place death's aftermath has consigned to her. I remember right after my father died I thought she'd want to step out into the world for herself, so I set up a checkbook for her and tried again and again to get her to take a trip with a church group. But she has wanted none of it, not the finances, not the travel. Often when she speaks about her life she slips into the past: *I've had a good life.* My desires for her are selfish, too. I'd love to feel like simply a daughter again. To walk in the door and sit down for a cup of tea with no other thought than to ask first about her day rather than to be thinking of the bills I have to look over and the calls that need to be made, even though at times, when her loneliness feels beyond reach, I hide in those duties.

I'd foreseen nothing of the places we'd all assume after my father's death. Maybe I'm surprised most of all by the way my mother has begun to grow closer to her earlier life, as if all other destinations have given way to old original paths. She won't venture far alone on the highway or up north to see her grandchildren, but she'll wind her way through the old tenement districts of Lawrence—though they are hardly the streets of her childhood—to do her errands at the Italian grocery and at the Italian bakery. Lawrence may be the place she still knows best in spite of nearly fifty years on this farm, where she kept to the house and yard. I don't ever remember her going for a walk into the woods or along the orchard here.

The stove, having run full all day, gave off a radiant warmth that spread through half the downstairs rooms. I filled it with wood and left my mother and aunt sitting beside it wrapped in their afghans. I bundled myself up in scarf and hat and parka, expecting a winter cold had come in with the setting sun, but as I stepped into the open night, I was surprised by the mildness of the air.

Safer than houses, I thought, the quiet road, the windless trees. As I crossed the peach orchard, the green glass votive I'd carried out with me cast a flickering light and made long shadows of the frail peach branches, and longer shadows of the white pines beyond. Shadows so distorted you couldn't tell the damaged trees from the unscathed ones. I turned full circle in the middle of the orchard, and I could discern in the

living-room window of my mother's house the faintest glow
from their candles. Besides the votive I carried with me, theirs
was the only human light I could see. The hills of Lawrence
were dark. Gone, the lamplit neighboring windows and the
long curve of streetlights going west and east. I couldn't even
make out the red radio beacon that I usually saw on the southern horizon.

I have lived in remote places and have seen night skies full
of the weight and lift of stars—so many stars there didn't seem
to be an inch between them—but I had never seen such a sky
above our farm. Here I was accustomed to nights paled by
city and suburban glow, and I had a moment's trouble finding
constellations—defiant Orion rising, the Pleiades, Cassio-
peia—I thought prominent in our half-starred sky. Now with
their familiarity drowned by the other stars, they seemed
smaller and part of a greater whole rather than the distinct
gatherings I'd always taken them for. Wonderful to see for
once. I felt we lived in a wilder, more remote place, and for
all the mildness of the night there seemed a greater distance
between outside and in. I couldn't help but think I stood in a
world closer to what we truly are, that with our lights we have
only thrown up the thinnest scrim, and tenuously disguised
how near we are to the night.

My own house was soaked with the cold. I wrapped myself in throws and odd blankets to read for a while amid all
that was dumb and useless: the oven, the faucets and sinks,
the lamps, the radiators, my computer, stereo, TV. Shapes no
longer having a function in that quiet. Funny to think if I were
to take them all away my rooms would be half-empty. And
without the sounds I'd long since become used to—the chuffs

141

of the furnace and refrigerator, the heat crackling in the radiators—I knew what I'd taken for silence was just an imitation of silence. All I could hear now were the few cars going by, fast and steady and purposeful—going somewhere—and I felt an immense distance between them and me. *There are those of the world*, they seemed to say, *and those not*.

After a few hours I returned to my mother's house to feed the fire. I called out as I entered, but, no matter how loudly I whispered their names, they lay too deeply asleep to hear. I bustled as much as I could to try to rouse them—I could be anyone!—and they didn't stir, not even when I opened the creaking stove doors to throw more wood on the fire. And though the house was far warmer than my own, I left them there, sleeping so faithfully, and returned to my bed where I dived fully dressed under the covers, my wool hat on my head. It was still dark when I heard the furnace and then the refrigerator click on and saw light from a downstairs lamp shed into the room. Almost instantly all the exaggerated feelings of the last day-and-a-half fell away and I was swallowed into the world again.

The storm had left no more than six inches of snow on the ground, yet we spent all winter cleaning up its debris. In every break in the weather folks hauled out their tools and set to work. There was a run on chainsaws at the hardware stores, and anyone with a chipper had small jobs for months. In the cemetery, I saw families taking turns with a hacksaw to clear the downed branches from the graves.

Come spring what's left of the scattered debris—the small branches and needle clusters, which seem so conspicuous and unsettling scattered on the snow—will begin to molder into the warming earth, and soon will be indistinguishable from the usual world. But I know the time will stay with me. For those thirty-two hours our own place had seemed so strange, but also so clearly defined as home. Now when I think of those hours, it's like the recollection of a tender dream.

16

White Clover

AFTER MIXED NEW ENGLAND WOODS ARE CLEAR-
cut for pulp, lumber, and cordwood, sometimes from a seeming nowhere the land sprouts pokeweed, bramble, white clover, or fireweed. They say the plants are from seeds that may
have been lying dormant for a century. The place would have
been a field then—pasture or meadow—and when the pines
and maples overtook the open land, their shade hampered the
germination of such light-loving plants. I imagine them small
as dust, the dormant seeds of clover, cradled in mineral earth
as the forested world passed into the soil—the fallen trunks
greening with lichen and softening as insects and mushrooms
work in, bringing them down to mix with pine needles, abandoned bark nests, and deer bones gnawed to dust. White clover, which had been buried along with the daily light of agriculture, now sun-warmed after so much time, sprouting
through fresh woodchips, leaf litter, and mold.

In 1919, with half its land under cultivation, Middlesex
County in northeastern Massachusetts ranked fifth in the
United States in the value of vegetables grown for market.
There were also twenty thousand milk cows, and almost
everyone knew the difference between Holsteins, Guernseys,

Ayrshires, Jerseys. Sour or sweet soil, late and early land, pasture, meadow, tillage. They worked with two-horse turning plows and teams of oxen, though farming had begun to enter its shiny, new stage: tractors also broke the spring soil and chemical fertilizers were coming into use. Yet by 1920, there were already a thousand fewer farms in the county than there had been in 1910—a decrease of over sixty-five thousand improved acres of land. Cultivation had been pushed farther and farther back from the terraces and drumlins of the Boston Basin, where market gardening had begun, and where there'd been fine soil for growing vegetables.

The decline of agriculture here is partly a story of the best land being lost to development, partly a story of the worst land being abandoned. And within those stories are all the singular stories of those caught in work. The blurred couple in front of their haywagon hardly had time to see the future. They were becoming obsolete with their particular tasks and endless chores: plowing, planting, haying, hoeing, cultivating, harvesting potatoes, storing carrots, thinning beets. The milking, mucking out the stalls, repairing the buildings and plows, shoeing the horses and oxen, clearing stones, clearing trees, the wood hauled out, cut and split and stacked, mending fence. Cooking pies and bread, three hot meals a day, canning tomatoes, beans, peas, peaches, making cheese, boiling sap, bottling milk. The clothes and beds, heating, testing, pressing the irons into the Sunday best, the floors to be scrubbed, the kitchen garden to be weeded, the children, the elderly, the sick. I remember still the day my aunt said, *I brought in so much wood as a child, I don't care if I ever see that Glenwood stove again.*

As the old-field woods are cleared, white clover sprouts its way into a world where farming is seen not in a daily light but a kindly one, like a language nearly lost and so practiced with all intention, and apart from a native understanding. Their chores have become our lost arts to be studied in schools for agriculture and classes for spinning and pie-making. Now that farms in the valley are vestigial, glimpsed in passing between industrial cities and suburban sprawl, the ones that are left have taken on a reverent sheen, sometimes precious and self-conscious. I know those driving by our farm see a landscape to admire and dream into, something settled and steeped with a history of family and work. *Don't ever sell,* they plead. *It's like an oasis.*

Our settled houses, the composure of our cared-for land and the woods beyond draw people's eyes because they remain. But how can we stand up under such a gaze? At times there seems to be such a wide gulf between who we are and who others see us as. And I don't want to let the last years stand for the whole, to let so many years of strength remain unremembered and unrecalled. At the accumulative end there should be voices insisting on the worth of all the days, even if—few remember anymore—farming was a life most of the country had walked away from.

On this second April after my father's death—the family having made it through one farming year without him—there are days I'm even hopeful for the future of this place, since David—a man who, all through his school years, worked for my father—will be coming back, at least for the coming season, to take care of the orchard and some of the fields and the farm stand. I had written to him in Ecuador where he was working in the Agricultural Program for the Peace Corps.

We'd made arrangements for the coming year by long slow-traveling letters—his written longhand by failing light, mine on a computer—or by telephone when he came down out of his village every once in a while. It was hard to believe we were in the same century when I talked to him. It felt like a leap of faith across more than miles—like a leap across time, when I imagined, or tried to imagine, where he was calling from: the cold, high country too steep for tractors, and too poor. Animals still working across the terraced hills, and travel between places largely on foot.

I don't know how long he'll stay on—he could do a thousand other things with his life. But he's here out of an old abiding loyalty, I think, to the farm he worked on all through his teens, all through college summers. *The best worker I ever had* I remember my father—not one to mete out praise—saying.

David wouldn't be returning from Ecuador until late in spring, so I was left to order some of the seed myself. For a few of the smaller crops I found my father's old orders scribbled on scrap paper: Avalanche cauliflower, Howden pumpkins, and Comet broccoli. I know he chose the cauliflower because it was self-blanching and the Howdens because of their thick skin and good weight, and I copied his order in both amount and variety. I felt safe in the measure of such things, imagining the long consideration of quality and yield, appearance, size, sweetness, and keeping qualities.

I know he stood by Lady Bell peppers for a long time, and with good reason, but this year there's been a nearly complete failure in the seed crop, so each customer has been restricted to one quarter ounce of seed. I spent hours this past January at the end of the day as the gray afternoons turned to dark, flip-

ping from one catalog to another—it's no help that the commercial catalogs offer more choices every year: hybrids, improved varieties, disease-resistant strains—looking for how
to make up the one more ounce of pepper seed we'll need,
weighing the attributes of blocky or long peppers, thin-
walled against thick, looking for old names I'd heard—anything familiar—comparing the days to germination between
one variety and the next, and marking down which ones are
early to color red. Who was I that I worried over a packet I
could pour into the palm of my hand, over something so
nearly weightless I could hold it out for the wind, or simply
blow it away like fine cold snow?

In the end I launched into what future I could imagine and
ordered eight kinds of peppers. There was safety in variety, I
reasoned, so I chose three different kinds of blocky green
bells: North Star, Yankee, King Arthur. I ordered Jalapeños
and Thai hot peppers, along with yellow and purple bells and
cubanelles. Then I went on to order other things we'd never
grown: tomatillos, baby eggplants, romanesco broccoli, and
tiny pear-shaped yellow tomatoes.

Not so much, these decisions, especially when I try to
imagine all the new seed that has taken root while clover lay
dormant. Seed carried in a bale of hay or caught on fur, or
dropped by birds. Winged seeds—light as chaff—blowing
in on a salty wind. Loosestrife, rank in the low places, snagged
on sheep's wool and washed into the river from the mills. Tomato seed brought in the pockets of Italians. The Polish wal-
nuts given by a Polish neighbor. All the years of my father's
Blue Hubbard squash carried down from what he'd chosen
and dried and saved every winter through fifty years. A jar of
the last, from two Novembers back, sits on his office shelf, la-

beled in his own hand, a part now—and reminder of—the simple past: *They were.* They were the ones who slept over cellars with carrots buried in sand and onions hung from a rafter, who kept whatever they judged best from one year to the next.

However much of the story disintegrates, won't some part survive in shards and remnants? Aren't there other dormancies—lying in wait among white clover and fireweed—which light alone won't raise? In some soils where flints and stone knives wash onto dirt roads after the rain, the story is almost beyond us. In others, it sours the land: French farmers turn over spent shells, barbed wire, and bones from the trenches. Our own fields turn up bits of ceramic—the handle of an ironstone cup or the clear blue-patterned rim of a porcelain plate. Glass from medicine bottles, too—cobalt blue or pale green —which have clouded like sea glass now. All minor notes and half steps with a few surges in the song. Enamel splinters from a painted red chair, cinders from doused fires, newsprint thinning, tearing, breaking up into smaller and smaller increments, until single letters mix with ash and clay and sand.

17

Twilight of the Apple Growers

THE EARLY NEW ENGLAND FARMS ALL HAD their apple trees that grew along a fence line or in a small block: stalwart, long-lived, their bearing limbs pruned to a craggy, turned grace. Apples—old workhorse crop—crushed for cider, dried beside the fire, and simmered into sauce. The late-ripening storage varieties—Baldwins, say—touched with frost, were packed away into March, and as the days lengthened their skins toughened then wrinkled, their flesh softened, and the dank, stone-sealed air of the apple cellar deepened to a winey depth.

In 1920, over a quarter million bearing apple trees had ranged across the drumlins and eskers of Middlesex County —far-spread full-sized trees producing more than a million bushels of fruit. We are so far from an agricultural economy now, I can't help but think at first that a million bushels of apples must have meant the early century was a propitious time for farming here, yet by then agriculture in New England had been in decline for years. Even by the mid-nineteenth century Henry Thoreau, walking his own corner of Middlesex County, could see the falling off: *None of the farmer's sons are willing to be farmers, and the apple trees are decayed, and the cellar holes are more numerous than the houses, and the rails are covered with lichens, and the old maids wish to sell out and move into the village, and have waited twenty years in vain for this purpose.... lands which the Indian long since was dispossessed of and now the farms are run out, and what were forests are now grain-fields, what were grain-fields, pastures.*

By the time my father planted his last orchard in the 1980s, apple growing in Middlesex County had diminished to little more than a thousand acres of orchards spread across seventy-four farms. In 1992, eight hundred and nineteen acres remained. Fifty-three farms. And they—tucked in among spreading suburbs and industrial complexes—are without context in the county or in the eastern part of Massachusetts. In tough weather—a droughty midsummer, say—when growers wonder how the apples will ever size up, they listen for news of rain in the beach and boating forecast, the rush hour weather, and weekend weather.

Our own farm claims little more than three hundred of the county's remaining apple trees. The main orchard, sloping behind the barns and houses and bordered on its far side by a stand of hundred-foot white pines, is hardly noticeable, except in blossom time, to a passerby. Most of the year our farm is dominated by the row crops—fields of corn and trellised tomatoes and vines of cucumbers and squashes, yet, even so, when I think of the possibility that all of it may pass away, it's the apple trees I can't imagine going—maybe because through all the changes here, there's always been an orchard.

In 1901 along with the house, the gradey herd of milking cows, the barn and its contents—pails, hammers, plows, scythes—my grandparents gained ownership of the Baldwins, Gravensteins, Red Astrakhans, and Ben Davis. A few of those trees hang on—thickset now, and crusted with lichen—in the far corners of the farm, but by mid-century most had been replaced by my father's plantings of McIntosh, Red Delicious, Cortland, and Northern Spy. By then he had sold the herd and had begun to concentrate on growing fruits and vegetables for the nearby citydwellers, hauling his produce to the corner markets in Lowell and Lawrence until the cities emptied of their prospects, the corner stores failed, and the world around us turned suburban.

As new ranches and split-levels were set down on old fields and in old woods, the traffic on our road became constant and we sold nearly all the produce we grew on our roadside stand. By then the varieties of apples we offered included Macoun, Jonah Reds, Paula Reds, a redder strain of Cortlands—red had become important in marketing—as the last orchard my father planted started to bear. Those trees cover only a few acres, but their wood is grafted to semi-dwarf rootstock, which means easier-to-pick smaller trees that produce higher yields per acre. Not so long-lived, they'll be replaced after a quarter-century or so, and will never look as tough and wind-staunch as the old Baldwin trees.

When most of the row crops have been plowed under and the fields are deep in rye, apples—like winter squash and pumpkins—bring in money after the killing frosts. Though they may extend the season, my father never counted apples among his most productive or lucrative crops. He always said corn was the draw. Even now, come July my mother will return from Sunday Mass saying, "All anybody wanted to know was when the corn would be ready." The stand opens with corn, and with the first sparse pickings everyone crowds the table and watches anxiously as a young boy tosses bushel after bushel on the table and packs the pile down into dozens and half dozens, they watch the dozens disappear and the bushels empty, afraid all will be gone before they get their turn. The stand—last stop on a Friday afternoon before the road to the beach, to the White Mountains, to the lake country in Maine—runs with corn all through the summer and the demand hardly lets up until summer itself lets up.

Never such a story for apples, which appear after corn, then tomatoes and peaches have contented everyone, and even the first astringent smell of the early Gravs and Paula Reds and Jerseymacs are lost when set beside the sweeter smells of peaches and cornsilk. Apples gain their true place in the cooler, drier air after Labor Day—the world back on its axis—when those who stop do so on the way home from work, or during a weekend morning in the middle of errands. *I love the smell of fall* some will say, as they breathe in the cold, sharp scent of apples. The first red leaves are falling one by one. The days are already growing brief.

If the scent of apples closes one year, pruning the orchard opens the next, bringing a kind of relief on the other side of winter restlessness: work to shake off the quiet contemplative months in a time not crowded by countless other chores and a shortness of time. Come late February or early March my father would take out his snips and saw and begin to work down the rows of the orchard. I like to remember him alone under the wide winter sky, studying the shape of each tree before making his cuts. He always liked to be doing something, even after the arthritis in his knees made it difficult to walk without the help of a cane. In his last years he'd drive his truck nearly from tree to tree. I can still see him as he'd pause after turning out of the seat to brace himself for the sure pain that would come when he put his weight on his knees. Down to bone on bone the doctor had said. Even so, he stayed with it—that was always his advice to me: *stay with it*—until he was eighty-five, his last spring, when he hired the man to prune the orchard for him.

After my father's death—the fields buried in snow—it was the dormant trees with their gray, turned branches that loomed large to me and made the farm feel like too much to care for. In the weeks afterwards, as I tried to square his affairs, I didn't give a thought to the summer row crops. I just wanted—beyond reason really—to see the orchard pruned as it had always been. I looked through all the cards and the several list-finders on his desk in an effort to find the name of that pruner he'd hired the spring before, and once I found the listing, heart in my throat, I called.

"I'd be glad to do it," he answered. "You've got a nice setup—an old romantic orchard. They don't make them that way anymore." He was glad to do it, and though his price was higher than my father ever would have ever settled on, I didn't know what else in the world to do but agree. In those months I'd probably have paid anything just for things to be the same. It was worth it to see him show up, snips and loppers in hand—strange with his radio, sunglasses, and wide-brimmed hat—on the first open day in late February. Even with all the corn snow still on the ground—we'd had over ten feet of it that winter—he worked deftly up and down the rows, and the shapes of the trees clarified in his wake.

Here is another spring. It's a late Wednesday afternoon and David and I are traveling west through the broad length of Middlesex and into more rural Worcester county on our way to the first Twilight Meeting of the year for apple growers. The interstate belies any sense of distance or towns-traveled-through as it cuts across the rolling, wooded hills of our region. The grasses are just starting to turn green, and the light feels a little milder as the sun slants toward the western hills, though the cold comes in quickly still.

We've both been pruning the orchard this year—Dave has taken a chainsaw to the tops of the older trees, while I've been working from the ground, pruning the lower limbs the best I know how, looking into the tangle of the crowns, trying to clear out what's growing down, or in, or crossing another branch. The watersprouts, the winter damage, the deer-bitten branch tips. You could hear me mumbling to myself: *That won't do any good—that should go—this one, maybe this.*

We still have a ways to go with the pruning even though the buds have been swelling for a while. As we left today for the Twilight Meeting—named so because it's held at the end of a workday—the buds, having already passed dormancy, silver tip, and green tip, were at the stage called half-inch green, when you can see the leafy folds just starting to break out. In the weeks to come will be tight cluster, pink, full bloom, petal fall, fruit set, then the June drop. Through all the variants of the April days—the warming trends, the cloudy, cold, gray setbacks, and the freak snows—the buds push forward towards their blossoming, softening the harsh winter forms of the trees. All the long months I've looked out on the severe turns of the long-pruned branches, and now at dusk, especially, the orchard feels full of peace, with the haze of incipient silver-white and green floating around the crowns of even the oldest, craggiest trees. For the moment they seem to be made only half of substance, and hardly bearers of fortunes and tradition.

The trees are clearly on our mind as we head into the Nashoba Hills. "I can't imagine the orchard paying for itself," I say casually.

"I know," Dave answers.

"Who will you get to pick all the apples?"

"I have no idea."

At the meeting there'll be apple growers from the northeastern region of Massachusetts, which includes Essex, Middlesex, and Worcester counties. Each meeting is held at a different host farm every month of the spring and early summer. The owner or manager leads a tour of his orchards, packing houses, and storage areas and afterwards the Extension agents from the University of Massachusetts Tree Fruit Program report on recent field trials and the insect migrations and hatches. They give out certification points for those with pesticide applicator's licenses.

The host farm this month is in the Nashoba Hills, which has always been the prime apple-growing region in the area and is where the largest orchards remain. The Soil Survey of 1924 praises the Charlton loam of these hills: *derived from glacial-till deposits which are commonly from 10 to 40 feet thick over the bedrock. This soil occurs on low, smooth, rounded, oblong or drumloid hills, and in many places caps the tops of ridges and hills having more or less stony hillsides.... Drainage is thoroughly established, but the soil has an excellent moisture-holding capacity, and crops rarely suffer even in dry seasons.... Apples do exceptionally well. The trees make a healthy growth, and the fruit is of good quality.*

As we turn off the interstate and approach the farm, the road is nearly swallowed by high round hills on either side. Slender dwarf trees cross them in soldierly rows, trees light and airy after their spring pruning. Though it's higher and colder here than at home, the green on these buds is breaking out, too. We pull into the parking lot of a broad, beamy, closed-for-the-winter farm stand. The windows are dark and bare, a fading *See You In The Spring* sign covers one of the doorpanes. The parking lot is filled with pickups. Some, high-riding shiny new four-wheel drives with elaborate detailing; others, rusting fenders and slatted wooden sides on the bed to give it some depth. On the doors, the orchard names: *Wheatley Orchards, Barstow Farms, Farms, Farms, Farms.*

We meet up with the others behind the farm stand in the apple storage area. There may not be many left but the apple growers range in prosperity and experience from a bewildered couple who've just bought into an old neglected orchard to third- or fourth-generation farmers who manage state-of-the art operations. Most are men in their fifties and sixties, some in their seventies. April is the time to finish up what pruning is left, and—just from work—they're dressed in workpants, jackets, peaked caps, and boots. They've already been working outside for months, so their cheeks are rough and red from the spring winds. There are a few women, and a scattering of younger men. We, with our five or six acres of orchard, half of which are aging, standard trees, belong with the smaller enterprises. Much of the meeting—the discussion of the breakdown of senescent fruit, comprehensive spray programs, and the shipping market—is banked towards larger growers and will be beyond our immediate concerns. Still, it feels like something we can't afford to miss.

Maybe there are forty or fifty of us gathered in a long hall that runs alongside the refrigeration areas. As I sit, I suddenly get a scent—round and deep—of long-stored apples, and, with the chill in the air, I forget the spring and feel for a moment as if winter is still to come. I remember the way the smell of apples filled our car when I was a child. On longer trips my father always traveled with a bag of apples on the floor behind the driver's seat. Northern Spies. When he pulled in for gas, if he had started in talking to the owner or attendant, he'd reach back and offer him an apple as he paid up.

I come around again to realize it's the scent of last fall's crop I now smell. The host pulls out a couple of stored samples to show how they've held up all these months. Beautiful, large, streaked with red. I remember the pruner telling me *Massachusetts apples are renowned outside Massachusetts— they're exported all over the world—McIntosh sell for a dollar apiece in England.* This time of year you'd find few in the nearby supermarkets, which are full of New Zealand Braeburns, Australian Granny Smiths, and Washington state Red Delicious. Oversized, a waxed shine, $1.19 a pound. Even if the Massachusetts crop failed completely, the supermarkets would still have their apples. Except for a few brief fall weeks imports always take up most of the alloted display space in the produce sections even as the early regional varieties—Paula Reds, Jerseymacs—appear in late August. No matter the flavor, people buy with their eyes, and everyone here would tell you those Washington state Red Delicious are meant for eyes alone.

Most of the men are large, and the tables feel a little crowded. Many haven't seen each other all winter, and there's a rumble of catch-up talk: *Retire, no, Christ, that's when they plant ya ... I was going to put out some oil next week, if it warms up a bit. Going to be a cold spring.* Many are talking about the cider situation. In recent years, several *E. coli* outbreaks have sent a scare through health officials and the public and now the rumors are all about requiring pasteurization for cider. No drops in the mix either, nothing that's touched the ground: *We might try running it through the milk pasteurizer. I tell you, regulations are what will kill us. It's ridiculous.*

The voices all feel familiar to me—this is the kind of talk I've overheard for much of my life. Still, I feel shy. I recognize a few old acquaintances of my dad. One or two step over to see me for a moment—"How's it going over there? How's your mother holding up?" "If I can be of some help ..." We talk politely for a few minutes until the conversation trails off, and they amble away to join another group.

The orchard tour is first, and the large lot of us pile into the backs of some of the pickups and jostle along the cart path to higher ground to look at some Galas that had been planted half a dozen years ago. The top of the hill is crowned with a nineteenth-century white clapboard homestead, which is shaded by a few ancient specimen apple trees long past production now. I guess they're what's left of an old orchard meant to span years and years. They, with their rough gray bark, more bullish trunk than crown, the new growth of long slim branches weeping towards the ground, make us almost believe such trees always were, and that it's we who are the first to change. But the idea of beauty that they suggest and that we hold—*old romantic orchards*—of trees planted in rows across open land, began only when apple growing became a deliberate occupation, going back no more than a few lifetimes. The earliest New England farmers tucked in wild apple trees where they could, and the result was nothing like the blocks and rows we've all come to know and love. Theirs was a disorder Thoreau loved and saw passing in his time:

I fear that he who walks over these hills a century hence will not know the pleasure of knocking off wild apples. Ah, poor man! there are many pleasures which he will be debarred from! Notwithstanding the prevalence of the Baldwin and the Porter, I doubt if as extensive orchards are set out today in this town as there were a century ago when these vast straggling cider-orchards were planted. Men stuck in a tree then by every wallside and let it take its chance. I see nobody planting trees today in such out of the way places, along almost every road and lane and wall-side, and at the bottom of dells in the wood. Now that they have grafted trees and pay a price for them, they collect them into a plot by their houses and fence them in.

So we also are aftercomers of a kind and cannot guess the beauty been.

"It's good to be up high," someone says, and it is, as I look west towards the Connecticut River Valley and the long blue of the greater hills. The sky is already deepening in the east. The cold sun, low in the west. Frail branches of the small trees cast long shadows. The farm manager talks about his Galas, his successes and failures, and as we stand among the trees some hang on his words, others look for themselves at the pruning job, or the way the buds are breaking. Then we trundle back down the hill to the storage house to drink coffee, eat hot dogs, and listen to the Extension agent from the Department of Plant and Soil Sciences give a rundown on rootstock trials and foliar calcium sprays for apples. Another takes his turn and discusses the oil spray schedule. Specific, scientific, where does such knowledge go beyond this room and these few people? An undertow of small talk begins to break out. It's been a long day, and attention is drifting away.

The agent brings us round by raising his voice a bit: "OK. Listen up. One last thing. The Pesticide Disclosure Act is in front of the Ag Committee in the House. I thought we had the Chair's support, but it doesn't look that way. Give a call. If this goes through it will require you to notify every abutter a week before every application. We'll have a hard time doing our job." His sense of urgency quiets the group down. Some pull out paper and scribble a note down. He gives them some numbers to call. One thing you can count on to make this crowd feel like a group again—themselves alone—is the threat of new regulations and legislation.

There isn't one here, I don't imagine, even the successful ones, who isn't staring off into the unknown. Farms have always been lost, more lost than ever revived. Middlesex county has been going certainly away from this way of life for a century and a half. The farmland here, with its cleared, well-drained soils, has been sought out for development for a long time, and when it passes from one generation to the next, unless it qualifies for special valuation, unless the children commit themselves to ten years of farming, the land is assessed for highest and best use, which prices it far beyond any agricultural future.

However uncertain, it's also true that those who remain must love the work—from the countless hours of pruning in the lengthening days of late winter to the final harvest in the brief days of autumn—even if it doesn't seem they've had a choice except to carry on from the ones who've gone before them. And some, maybe many, who love it have not survived for a thousand reasons—family, finances, hard luck among them. But in a world of choices whoever doesn't love it has no chance at all. Next meeting, next month, in a longer twilight, in warmer air, the apples will be in pink, and it will be a busier time for work, though most who are here will attend that meeting also.

After the last talk dies down everyone drifts off to the parking lot. I stand at our truck waiting for David who's stayed behind to talk to one of the Extension agents. I look back at the storage house where we all met, and the building suddenly seems overlit in the growing dark. I can hear bits of conversation in the distance. *They're saying frost in the lower valleys. Can you still take care of my cider apples this year? Let's talk about it before next meeting.* Yes, if, when it goes, all the particular talk will go, too. The words and their fullest meanings: *petal fall, fruit set, June drop. Stay with it.* The last truck doors slam shut.

It's after the evening commute so the road is quiet, and the birds are already silent. The silver-green tips of the apple trees, glinting. Lights go out in the storage house. One by one I can hear the engines turn over and the trucks drive off. Silence. A lingering sting of gasoline in the air, then the smell of the spring buds returns.

18

A Tour of the Farm Stands

Though we have many substantial houses of brick or stone, the prosperity of the farm is still measured by the degree to which the barn overshadows the house.

—THOREAU

THESE DAYS, IN THE COUNTIES SURROUNDING Boston, the prosperity of the farm is measured by the degree to which the farm stand overshadows the house. And the prominence of such farm stands is a true marker of the changes in agriculture here since Thoreau's time. Thoreau, of course, was being critical: *To what end, pray, is so much stone hammered? In Arcadia, when I was there, I did not see any hammering stone. Nations are possessed with an insane ambition to perpetuate the memories of themselves by the amount of hammered stone they leave. . . .* But when I gaze at the photographs of the linked buildings that were once this farm, turned in on themselves to keep out the wind, ending in an outsized white barn far larger than the house, I don't think of ambition so much as I think of a sturdy, self-contained world that spoke for hope.

With the barn gone, the remaining house and carriage shed

form a modest L. When I knock at, then enter the side door to bring my aunt some of the first corn of the year or a cupful of peas, the two-hundred-year-old rooms—hushed except for the ticking clocks—feel separate and seemingly far from everything else on the farm today, the true workings of which—packing house, the greenhouse, and the storage buildings for machinery—are across the road from where she lives. There haven't been overcrowded noonday meals around the dining-room table for years now that most of the workers, who eat their sandwiches in the packing shed or in back of the stand, are hired out of Lawrence or Lowell.

The farm stand itself appears solid and on its own some distance from the house. It's separate even from my memories of the quiet, three-sided shack we first called the farm stand, which I tended as a child, where we sold a few bushels of corn and a basket of tomatoes and beans on a summer day. Almost separate, too, from our practical old customers who are dwindling: the ones looking for green tomatoes every September and bushels of pickling cukes, the old Italians coming out from Lawrence for boxes of canning tomatoes, cheap in the late August glut, the Lebanese women looking for kousa, a dozen or two or three all the same size, so they'll cook evenly. Mixing with the old Italians and Lebanese are the newcomers in town who've settled in the houses on old fields, and the newcomers to the cities—Hispanic and Cambodian families—looking for hot peppers and shell beans.

They walk into a broader, beamier place than in the past, a place aproned by a paved parking space. In season the double doors are propped open, greeting and calling the passing world, and window boxes and half-barrels brim with impatiens or petunias or marigolds. After the punishing summer heat passes, pumpkins, apples, and bunched cornstalks are ranged across its front. We've always opened for business in mid-July with the first of the corn, and we've closed right after Halloween—a straggle of pumpkins unsold, some apples and squash to wholesale.

When the farm stand closes its doors to the winter, the place itself appears as strangely plain as the fields that are planted in winter rye. There's the last lingering scent of pears on the air. I've heard, in the waning days of October, our own customers say *I wish you were open all year*. What I think they really mean is that they'd rather the growing season was far less brief. Sixty days of tomatoes, seventy-five days of corn hardly seem enough when all is said and done, and when the fall stars are burning out of the summer haze, no other flavor is so greatly desired as what has just passed.

It makes economic sense now, though, to think about extending the season beyond the hundred days of corn and pumpkins and apples in order to have some cash flow early, and then late—something many farm stands in the region have already done, bringing in produce and bedding plants in early spring, then Easter lilies, and hanging plants for Mother's Day. They keep going all the way to Christmas trees and poinsettias, and are busier than ever, the demand for the aura of the rural life being all that much greater as the available farmland continues to shrink.

So on this raw, rainy afternoon in mid-May, David and I have set out on the road to look at some other farm stands—to see how they're set up, to see what they carry in the early season. I've charted a route north and west of us where I know there are half a dozen larger farms, and we've set out across the Merrimack into the low hill country of southern New

Hampshire. Once across the river, through the city of Nashua and beyond the worst congestion of the Boston commute, the road starts to wind through open country—fields, mixed woods, white pine, some hemlock—and small towns, white with their churches set on high ground, old local mills and a small river running through, where the teasel still may be growing wild. Our own town, cramped and crammed with its spill out of both mill cities, with its proximity to Boston, hasn't looked like this for years. The farther we go, the steeper the terrain becomes: more woods, the country a little wilder, the growing season a little shorter. Though even here, on the roads between town centers, newer houses on broad bare lots are sprouting up on once-open land.

The apple trees are blossoming now in the late, wet spring. The whole spring has been so cool that every kind of blossom is lasting a long time, and the blooming seasons of different trees and shrubs are growing into one another rather than giving way—the forsythias, still bright yellow as the lilacs begin to open out. It makes for a fragrant air. Who doesn't love the work now, before the summer pests, the heat, the actuality of the crop—for now it is all possibility—will never love it. We pass a crew in oilers setting out lettuce on some early land. A field planted in peas. "Further along than ours," says Dave. I think of my dad and the way when he was driving anywhere he would notice the farms in the landscape more than anything. He seemed to be able to spot them anywhere, in places where no one else would think to look. He'd see the hint of an orchard behind a screen of pines, or a squash field between office buildings.

The first stand we stop at is as large as they come around here and I'm guessing it must be open most of the year. Barn rustic. Hanging plants are hooked along the eaves—geraniums and impatiens. Its front is full of bedding plants—pansies and perennials—set on low benches along the front. The pansies are the showiest with the bold purples and the yellows of their pie faces. The perennials are still a lock of promise, though the damp day has brought out the scent of lavender—a popular plant these days—spicy and clean.

Almost no native vegetables or fruits are ready yet. Asparagus and rhubarb are the only early New England choices, so the displays of fresh produce in the interior of the stand are full of imported fruits and vegetables: California artichokes, avocados, peaches, Florida citrus, Holland tomatoes. Even the apples are from away, and heavily waxed. They may be of higher quality than can be found in the local supermarkets, but they are also much more expensive. And the blueberries are five dollars a pint. David raises his eyebrows. I can imagine one of the white-haired women who come weekly to our stand, leaning on her cane to pick up the berries, looking hard at the price. She'd set them quickly back down again, and inspect everything more hesitantly afterwards.

More than a hundred days, and you're really just another kind of merchant. The shelves above the produce bins are stocked with jams, jellies, preserves, and conserves whose names always conjure the rural—*Weathervane Farms, Greenwood Farms, Molly's Kitchen*—and whose labels are adorned with etchings of workhorses and moldboard plows or specimen oaks. Candles, cookies, breads, candies. Lavender, statice, strawflower wreaths on the walls, and bundles of dried oregano, thyme, and bay hanging from the beams. Even as I'm wondering who buys all this, I jot down some brand names and addresses off the bottles of goods on the shelves.

We look at the way the bins are constructed, and at the little greenhouse warts the stands have on them, talk about how to construct them, how to make the most of a small space, where to place the shelves. I see rusted farm implements resting on the rafters. Saw blades and ice tongs hang on the walls. We all make the most of the past. Even though most of the produce is from other places, the stand smells familiar, as always, with its scent of old wood and potting soil, and something green and astringent like parsley or celery.

As we continue on down the back roads from farm stand to farm stand, we can't help but separately wonder what our own place will become. Dave and I joke about a future of doughnuts, hayrides, ice cream, a petting zoo. He recalls how a neighboring farmer attested: *We made money on the pumpkins, sure, but we made more on the candy apples and popcorn and sausage sandwiches.* Today we've stopped at places that have llamas, sheep, a few ducks. They host birthday parties for children. The name of the occupation has changed: husbandryman, farmer, grower, retailer. Creeping in are words like agro-entertainment and agro-tourism.

The last farm stand I'd marked on our route was a little farther north on the other side of the river. There are few places to cross the Merrimack, and most bridges are in the heart of the old mill cities so we have to jog through the narrow streets of Nashua in order to cross, sensing our way to the river by looking for millstacks and low land until we catch a glimpse of the waters that were once described, at the height of industrial pollution in the sixties, as too thick to pour, too thin to plow.

"In Ecuador, sometimes you'd have to travel for hours just

to cross the river." Dave had only been back here a month, and sometimes his mind seemed alive with two places at the same time. His world had grown thick with its crossings and accretions and comparisons. "People talk so much here. In my village, people would spend the whole rainy afternoon together, six men, two playing cards, four watching, and not a word between them." As David remembers—and I imagine—Ecuador, the far shore appears open and green.

We turn north and travel a road that runs parallel to the river's east bank along the crest of a small hill. To our left we can look across to river valley land that sweeps down to the Merrimack's edge. In places there are new colonials standing square on their lots, without landscaping, and yet without furnishing or curtains so you can see clear through the twelve-light windows to the river beyond. They've been built on even, stoneless, rich soils, on what had been some of the best farmland left in the area, something like the Ondawa fine sandy loam of our part of the valley: *this land is easily plowed and cultivated, coming readily into good tilth.... The overflow in spring is depended on in a measure to keep up fertility. Comparatively small deposits are made by the streams of this region at flood time. Crops are rarely damaged by floods, which occur when little or nothing is growing on the land.*

We arrive at the last farm stand—a refurbished long barn with a forthright simplicity—a few minutes before six, just at closing time. The river runs straight and swift in back, the fields are planted right up to the parking lot. With our arrival comes a little flurry of activity as people stop on the way home from work. Most have come for asparagus, maybe enough potatoes to tide them over, and their purposeful errands remind me of the way our own stand sometimes feels in the waning days of the season. I imagine however much is ordered and sold from away and beyond, any farm can still at times be a world of its own, with its talk about the harvested frosted heads of cabbage, or the first peas of the season, talk entirely local and our own even as, above us, crossing and recrossing the sky, satellites map the earth. We walk through the bedding plants. I buy some asparagus.

As we begin our journey back on the same road I keep my eyes on the river running behind the new houses. The braided, swift waters must be the breakup of the last stubborn ice of winter—just now dissolving into water and flowing into daylight—that had lain under shadowed hemlock woods in the White Mountains. The road continues to hug the river, and I begin to realize we must be traveling on the road Thoreau and his brother could see in a moment's rest from their river journey at the end of summer in 1839: *The open and sunny interval still stretched away from the river, sometimes by two or more terraces, to the distant hill country, and when we climbed the bank we commonly found an irregular copse-wood skirting the river, the primitive having floated down stream long ago to—the "King's navy." Sometimes we saw the river road a quarter or half a mile distant, and the particolored Concord stage, with its cloud of dust, its van of earnest travelling faces, and its rear of dusty trunks, reminding us that the country had its places of rendezvous for restless Yankee men. There dwelt along at considerable distances on this interval a quiet agricultural and pastoral people, with every house its well, as we sometimes proved, and every household, though never so still and remote it appeared in the noontide, its dinner about these times. There*

they lived on those New England people, farmer lives, fa-
ther and grand-father and great-grandfather, on and on with-
out noise, keeping up tradition and expecting, beside fair
weather and abundant harvest, we did not learn what.

And as we travel along the road they saw from the river, I
think of how impossible their journey would be now, our
lives as far from theirs, surely, as theirs were from Passaconaway's. Thoreau and his brother camped where they docked
and knocked at houses to ask about buying a loaf of bread, a
melon from the field, a drink from the well. They slept in the
open at any sheltered place along the bank. What would we
make of them if they were to come to our doors now, asking
for bread, travel-scuffed, out of nowhere?

For Thoreau, there were worlds to lament, the world of
river freight was passing, the canal locks were falling into disuse as the railroads took trade off the rivers. A world we don't
know to miss anymore, the river having changed so since,
having become an industrial commodity for the mill cities
whose bricks were shipped down on the water, and the mill
cities having died away, and commerce and industry both
leaving the Merrimack as surely as salmon and sturgeon.

When he sailed the river my ancestors lived in the hills of
Italy and Lebanon, and spoke no English, and there wasn't
even the rumor of work that would bring my grandparents to
Lawrence. The crest stones were set on the Lawrence dam as
he labored at Walden over drafts of *A Week on the Concord
and Merrimack Rivers,* setting down what he desired—what
anyone might desire—our lives to be: *The frontiers are not
east or west, north or south, but wherever a man fronts a fact,
though that fact be his neighbor, there is an unsettled wilder-*

ness between him and Canada, between him and the setting sun, or, further still, between him and it. Let him build himself a log-house with the bark on where he is, fronting IT, and wage there an Old French war for seven or seventy years, with Indians and Rangers, or whatever else may come between him and the reality, and save his scalp if he can.

As his words cross with the immigrant accounts still swirling in my head, I can't help but feel the gap between what has been of so many lives along this river—*Keep on going and going till night, keep on doffing all the time, fast and fast. Come! The boss is to come. Come on, are you still there?*—and what we have hoped our lives to be as we build on what's crumbled to dust and changed beyond reckoning, the rusting mill gates and the collapsed barn, build on the ruins of those who have been forced away, those who have walked away from home and past homes and beyond the river murmuring, glimpsing, gone.

My own imaginings send tremors—like flawed glass, prismatic—through every solid thing I see. Smoke and snow distort; and petal fall, and voices tumbling through the years. It's the voices that leave as much as hammered stone, and all who've been voiceless, all whose tongues were uncomprehended, whose experience has been answered with silence. Always the hope is that somewhere in time they will finally be understood—all the declarations and questions, and what is still so much beyond speech, or too elusive for speech: *Got in three loads . . . Got in four loads . . . A hard wind blow . . . I have got the most of my wool spun and two webs wove. . . . Sometimes we did not have enough to buy bread one day or two days. . . . Come, the boss is to come. . . . Are you still there? . . . Resolved, that as the laborer is worthy of his hire, the price for labor shall be sufficient.... What did we know of the war.... We saw churches and gravestones smashed to dust.... We knew it was serious but we didn't know how serious.... And I gave place to them, I that can make the dry leaf turn green again.... Peace, peace is the last wish ... It droppeth as the gentle rain upon the place beneath.... Who's going to be farming in this valley ten years from now?*

My father's gravelly, practical, last voice has joined all the others of a valley seen new each time, the way Thoreau saw his own trip once in the journey, twice in the words found to write of it, and yet again as he lay dying at the age of forty-four. His recollections labored over, layered over, to join with a present day. Forty-four years old—more than three of his lifetimes fit between then and now. His trip down the river had been the striking out of a young man, the retelling of the trip had been an elegy for his brother, dead at twenty-nine. When, in his own last days, his sister read aloud the passage he'd written of the long swift journey home past Nashua and into Lowell with the first autumn wind at their backs, the story goes he smiled at the remembrance of it, and whispered *now comes good sailing.*

I keep thinking of Thoreau and the lives of the valley as David and I, in order to avoid the last of the city traffic, veer away from the river and cut into the back way over the hill roads—Jeremy Hill, Bush Hill, Marsh Hill Road—that ride the contours of the valley. One moment we have a high clear view, the next we're nestled in wooded low places. No matter the names for them and their meanings—drumlins, eskers, terraces, hills—they are all the work of glaciers, and of time, are the soils that swirl in the survey maps—Coloma fine sandy soil, Hinckley, Merrimack—whose fugitive colors not so long ago charted each place here for its agricultural purpose.

This May evening is the coolest in a long time. We pass through most of the last of the farmland and open land, more fields and farms and woods than you'd believe from the main roads and the river roads. Is this an illusory way home or the real way home? Or one of many? Smoke rises out of the last fires of winter. Here and there windows are open to the fresh air. Even with the cold and gray—it has been gray since November—two or three times today I've overheard people say *everything's so green*. Beside me, Dave is running over with ideas about the early season. As he talks about putting up a greenhouse for some early tomatoes and maybe trying some bedding plants, a teeming rain falls soundlessly on the windshield. The roadside branches, stained dark and dripping; the last light, leaving the woods and the dense tangle of black alder, maple, and pine. We come up to the edge of the farm just at the old apple orchard—now comes good sailing—and see the blossoms lighting the dusk.

NOTES

PAGE 1 Epigraph, part I: *The Selected Letters of Emily Dickin-son*, Thomas H. Johnson, editor (Cambridge: The Belknap Press, 1958), p. 141.

PAGE 16 The information on soils in chapter 2 and throughout the book have been derived from *Soil Survey of Middlesex County, Massachusetts, Series 1924*, United States Department of Agriculture and the Massachusetts Department of Agriculture.

PAGE 19 *The quality of mercy:* Shakespeare, *The Merchant of Venice*, act IV, scene 1, lines 190–92.

PAGE 23 "Marching Through Georgia," by Henry C. Work.

PAGE 24 The statistics in chapter 3 and throughout on farming in the nineteenth century have been derived from *Soil Survey of Middlesex County, Massachusetts, Series 1924*. The information on milk inspections here and in chapter 4 has been derived from *The Report of the Lawrence Survey* (Lawrence, MA: Trustees of the White Fund, 1912). The survey was commissioned by the trustees of the White Fund to look into living conditions and the state of public health in the city of Lawrence. See "Part II: Public Health," by Frank Sanborn, pp. 147–216.

The quotes in this chapter concerning the conditions of milk farms are from the captions to photographs within these pages. A map of the Lawrence milk supply is published in the report.

PAGE 25 *As we rode along:* Silas Coburn, *History of Dracut* (Lowell, MA: The Courier-Citizen Press, 1922), from an account by George Mozley, pp. 180–81.

PAGE 27 *was born in Ireland: The Lawrence Telegram,* Lawrence, MA, November 11, 1918.

PAGE 51 Epigraph, part II: Henry David Thoreau, *A Week on the Concord and Merrimack Rivers* (Orleans, MA: Parnassus Imprints, 1987), p. 191.

PAGE 54 *It was already:* Thoreau, *A Week,* p. 100.

PAGE 55 *All along the river:* William Wood, *New England's Prospect* (Amherst: University of Massachusetts Press, 1977), p. 64.

being the first: John Pendergast, *The Bend in the River* (Tyngsboro, MA: Merrimack River Press, 1991), from a Contact Period map reproduction, p. 78.

PAGE 57 *The living were in no wise:* Pendergast, *The Bend in the River,* p. 43.

unmapped, unmarked: Howard S. Russell, *Indian New England Before the Mayflower* (Hanover, NH: University Press of New England, 1980), p. 201.

it was thought by some: Thoreau, *A Week,* p. 263.

PAGE 59 *haste to get past the village:* Thoreau, *A Week,* p. 306.

At the time of our voyage: Thoreau, *A Week,* pp. 306–307.

PAGE 62 *Our hands are soldiers' property:* Excerpt from a letter of Dorothy Dudley of Cambridge, Massachusetts, in Catherine

Fennelly, *Textiles in New England 1790–1840* (Meriden, CT: Meriden Gravure Co., 1961), p. 3.

For the section on the spinning wheel collection at the Museum of American Textile History, I am indebted to Joan Whittaker Cummer's *A Book of Spinning Wheels* (Portsmouth, NH: Peter E. Randall, 1993).

"They say a humming wheel rises": See Jane C. Nylander, *Our Own Snug Fireside* (New Haven: Yale University Press, 1994), p. 175. Francis Underwood describes the work of spinning: "Then, while the hum of the wheel rises to a sound like the echo of wind in a storm, backwards she steps, one, two, three . . ."

PAGE 64 *I have got the most of my wool spun:* From a letter of Malenda Edwards, in Thomas Dublin, ed., *Farm to Factory* (New York: Columbia University Press, 1981), pp. 86–87.

PAGE 67 *Since our voyage:* Thoreau, *A Week*, p. 264.

PAGE 68 *The English came:* Coburn, *History of Dracut*, pp. 38–39.

PAGE 69 *At first, the sight of so many bands:* Benita Eisler, ed., *The Lowell Offering: Writings by New England Mill Women (1840–1845)* (New York: Harper and Row, 1977), p. 180.

PAGE 70 *There are girls here for every reason:* Eisler, ed., *The Lowell Offering*, pp. 60–61. This excerpt is from "The Letters of Susan," composed by Harriet Farley for publication in *The Lowell Offering*. "Mother-in-law" refers to a person we would call a stepmother today.

PAGE 71 *One would swear:* Charles Dickens, *American Notes for General Circulation* (Boston: Ticknor and Fields, 1867), p. 76.

You ask if the work: Eisler, ed., *The Lowell Offering*, from "The Letters of Susan," p. 53.

PAGE 72 *The Overseers:* Eisler, ed., *The Lowell Offering,* from the Regulations for the Appleton Company, p. 25.

I have sometimes stood: Eisler, ed., *The Lowell Offering,* from "The Letters of Susan," p. 57.

Chairs, chairs: Eisler, ed., *The Lowell Offering,* from "The Letters of Susan," p. 73.

It is now: Eisler, ed., *The Lowell Offering,* from "The Letters of Susan," pp. 55–56.

PAGE 73 *I also wish you could see a prairie: The American Agriculturist,* vol. 1, no. 1, April 1842, pp. 14–15. The excerpt is from a letter to the editor entitled "Something about Western Prairies," by Solon Robinson.

PAGE 74 *The children of New England:* Quoted in Eisler, ed., *The Lowell Offering,* p. 11.

Lowell Hall was always: Eisler, ed., *The Lowell Offering,* pp. 32–33. From the comments of Professor A. P. Peabody, who lectured every winter for the Lowell Lyceum.

PAGE 75 *I had closed my book:* Eisler, ed., *The Lowell Offering,* p. 209.

PAGE 77 *At the time I was just about fourteen:* Transcribed from the tape "The Lawrence Textile Strike: Viewpoints on American Labor," produced by Myles Jackson (New York: Random House, 1971).

PAGE 78 *And it was hot:* Mary H. Blewitt, *The Last Generation: Work and Life in the Textile Mills of Lowell, Massachusetts 1910–1960* (Amherst, MA: University of Massachusetts Press, 1990), p. 111.

PAGE 79 *They had advertised:* Tamara K. Hareven and Randolph Langenbach, *Amoskeag: Life and Work in an American*

Factory-City (Hanover, NH: University Press of New England, 1978), p. 221.

PAGE 80 *The spinning room:* Hareven and Langenbach, *Amoskeag*, pp. 127, 129.

PAGE 81 *Everybody got only so much black cloth:* Hareven and Langenbach, *Amoskeag*, p. 216.
    There were so many black frames: Hareven and Langenbach, *Amoskeag*, p. 189.
    My work was handlooms: Hareven and Langenbach, *Amoskeag*, p. 206.
    We tied each end with a knot: Blewitt, *The Last Generation*, pp. 77–78.

PAGE 82 *They never wanted to see a loom stop:* Blewitt, *The Last Generation*, p. 87.
    And it was gloomy: Blewitt, *The Last Generation*, p. 111.

PAGE 84 *You didn't dare ... They'd come around to your house:* Transcribed from "The Lawrence Textile Strike: Viewpoints on American Labor."

PAGE 86 The testimonies of strikers are drawn from *Report on Strike of Textile Workers in Lawrence, Mass. in 1912*, prepared by Chas. P. Neill, Government Printing Office, Washington D.C., Document no. 870. These excerpts are taken from the testimony of Samuel Lipson, pp. 32–41; Charles Dhooghe, pp. 157–59; Auguste Wante, pp. 147–49; and John Boldelar, pp. 153–55.

PAGE 89 The discussion of "The Internationale" is transcribed from "The Lawrence Textile Strike: Viewpoints on American Labor."

PAGE 90 *the eloquence of an Italian:* Transcribed from "The Lawrence Textile Strike: Viewpoints on American Labor."

   This human being: Excerpt from Joseph Ettor's speech in front of the Lawrence City Council.

   I sent my child away: From the testimony of Samuel Lipson, *Report on Strike of Textile Workers,* p. 44.

PAGE 94 Chapter 11, "Influenza, 1918," owes much to Alfred Crosby's *America's Forgotten Pandemic: The Influenza of 1918* (Cambridge: Cambridge University Press, 1989). I am indebted to the Immigrant City Archives Historical Society of Lawrence in Lawrence, Massachusetts, where I was able to consult the Records of the Board of Health, January 1918 to April 1931, and the Board of Health Influenza Journal, 1918 to 1920. In addition, the Archives houses recordings of oral histories. Listening to these voices helped in my understanding of the atmosphere of the time. The recordings made of the recollections of Daniel Murphy and Sister Jeanne D'Arc were particularly helpful. Also useful were copies of the *Lawrence Telegram* and the *Lawrence Sun American,* September to November, 1918.

PAGE 105 The title and epigraph of chapter 12, "The Pure Element of Time," are taken from the opening chapter of Vladimir Nabokov's *Speak, Memory* (New York: Vintage, 1989).

   I'd be walking to Lowell High: Blewitt, *The Last Generation,* p. 307.

PAGE 106 *You go up and down the aisle:* Hareven and Langenbach, *Amoskeag,* p. 381.

PAGE 108 *When I talk about my work:* Hareven and Langenbach, *Amoskeag,* pp. 201–202.

PAGE 112 *Below the Lawrence Falls:* Transcribed from the recorded interview with Ernie Russell conducted by the Immigrant City Archives of Lawrence, MA. Tape #303, Counter Nos. 111–19.

PAGE 113 The section on the Ayer Clock owes a debt to Octavio Paz's poem "I Speak of the City," *The Collected Poems of Octavio Paz 1957–1987*, Eliot Weinberger, ed. (New York: New Directions, 1991), pp. 510–17. The facts of the clock restoration were drawn from Jeanne Schinto, *Huddle Fever* (New York: Knopf, 1995). See pp. 279–84.

PAGE 116 *It's been tough: The Boston Globe*, December 13, 1995, p. 37.

PAGE 117 Epigraph, part III, from "At the Fishhouses" by Elizabeth Bishop, *The Complete Poems 1927–1979* (New York: Farrar, Straus, and Giroux, 1979), p. 66.

PAGE 123 *As we glided over:* Thoreau, *A Week on the Concord and Merrimack Rivers*, pp. 93–94.

PAGE 127 *How can something be good:* "Path of the Pipeline's Progress," *The Boston Sunday Globe*, December 7, 1997, pp. B16–B17.

PAGE 128 *we all think:* From *Twenty-Four Conversations With Borges: Interviews by Roberto Alifano, 1981–1983* (Housatonic, MA: Lascaux Publishers, 1984), p. 12.

PAGE 136 *It is strange:* From Anton Chekhov's short story, "Gusev."

PAGE 144 Current farming statistics in Middlesex County, Massachusetts, in chapter 16, "White Clover," and in succeeding chapters, have been derived from a 1992 agricultural census conducted by the United States Department of Agriculture.

Information on seed survivors such as white clover was gleaned from *A Sierra Club Naturalist's Guide, Southern New England* by Neil Jorgensen (San Franscico: Sierra Club Books, 1978). See pages 211–13.

PAGE 150 *None of the farmer's sons:* From *The Journal of Henry David Thoreau*, Bradford Torrey and Francis H. Allen, eds. (Boston: Houghton Mifflin, 1906), vol. 3, pp. 237–38.

PAGE 160 *I fear that he:* From Thoreau's journal entry for November 16, 1850.

PAGE 163 *Though we have:* Thoreau, *Walden and Civil Disobedience* (New York: Viking Penguin, 1983), p. 100.
To what end, pray: Thoreau, *Walden*, pp. 100–101.

PAGE 170 *The open and sunny interval:* Thoreau, *A Week*, p. 266.

PAGE 171 *The frontiers are not:* Thoreau, *A Week*, pp. 379–80.

ACKNOWLEDGMENTS

Acknowledgment is due to the publications where some of these essays appeared: *The Georgia Review* originally published "Afterwards," "Baldwins," and "Influenza 1918," which was later reprinted in *Best American Essays, 1996*. *The Georgia Review* also published the first serializations of "Twilight of the Apple Growers" and (under the title "The Wilderness North of the Merrimack") an adaptation of "The Quality of Mercy" and "By Said Last Named Land." "Last Look" was originally published in a slightly different form as "The New Pruner" in *Orion*.

I'd like to thank the staff at Immigrant City Archives in Lawrence, in particular Ken Skulski and Mary Armitage, for their invaluable guidance. Thanks also to Sarah Blake and Kathy Aponick for their close attention to the manuscript in its final form, to Elizabeth Brown for her help with musical research and her attention to detail, to Blake Tewksbury for the loan of his family's Farmer's Diary.

Gratitude, always, to the MacDowell Colony for providing me with a quiet place to work, and to Stanley Lindberg at *The Georgia Review* for his continued support over the years. Special thanks and gratitude to Deanne Urmy at Beacon Press for her clear-eyed faith in these pages.

Library of Congress Cataloging-in-Publication Data

Brox, Jane, 1956–
    Five thousand days like this one : an American
    family history / Jane Brox.
        p.   cm. — (A Concord library book)
    ISBN 0-8070-2106-7 (cloth : acid-free paper)
    1. Brox, Jane, 1956–   —Family.   2. Brox family.
3. Family farms—Merrimack River Valley (N.H. and
Mass.)   4. Farm life—Merrimack River Valley (N.H. and
Mass.)   5. Merrimack River Valley (N.H. and Mass.)—
Biography.   I. Title.   II. Series
CT274.B779B758   1999
974.2'7204'0922—dc21
    [B]   98-35051

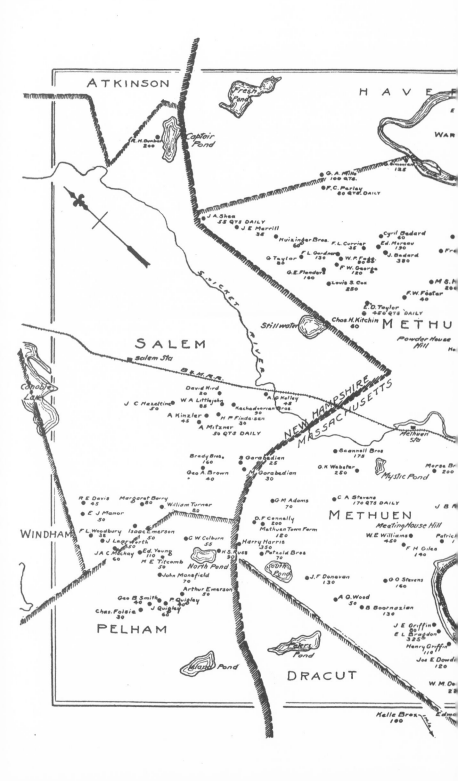